COMMON SENSE
IN MUSIC TEACHING

Also by Dr. WILLIAM LOVELOCK

A Concise History of Music
9th printing

The Rudiments of Music
5th printing

A Student's Dictionary of Music
2nd Printing

Elements of Orchestral Arrangement

Elementary Accompaniment Writing

Published by BELL

COMMON SENSE
IN MUSIC TEACHING

by

WILLIAM LOVELOCK
D.Mus. (London)

G. BELL AND SONS LTD
LONDON

First Edition 1965
Reprinted 1973

Published by
G. Bell and Sons Ltd
York House
Portugal Street
London, WC2A 2HL

Printed in Great Britain by
Billing & Sons Limited, Guildford and London

Contents

Acknowledgement

Not for the first time my sincere thanks go to Dr. W. Dunwell for his kindness in reading the first draft of this book and for his cogent and helpful comments.

W. L.
Brisbane, April, 1964

I

Introductory

In a notice of a former publication of mine an erudite reviewer remarked that 'you can call Dr. Lovelock either honest or barefaced'. In the improbable event of his reviewing the present book he might feel inclined to add the epithet 'blunt'. Whether or not I may appear at times unduly blunt is a matter of opinion; but there are things which need to be stated categorically, things which if 'wrapped up' for fear of giving offence would lose their impact. Any bluntness of expression which the reader may find is intended to hammer home what seem to me to be important points, or points which teachers are too often apt to overlook.

It is not, admittedly, usual to employ the personal pronoun in what purports to be a serious text-book, but since I have in some instances drawn from and quoted my own personal experience as teacher and examiner, it seemed simpler and certainly less cumbersome to use 'I' rather than 'the writer'. Also for the sake of simplicity I have consistently used 'he' or 'him' or 'his' when 'he or she', etc., would be more strictly accurate.

Colloquialism, too, is not usually considered appropriate in a book of this kind, but it often helps to clarify points in a simple manner. It also helps in actual teaching. More than one student has told me that he wished I would write my books in the same style of language as I use in personal teaching. I only wish I dared do so. But I could envisage much raising of academic eyebrows if, in a passage on three-part writing, I were to use such an expression as 'now we cook up the alto'; or to suggest, in dealing with rhythmic control in performance, that the player should 'whack the beats out in his head'.

This book is addressed primarily to the less experienced teacher as well as to the candidate for a teacher's diploma and consequently does not attempt to deal with any advanced aspects of technique, etc. It aims to help the kind of teacher who is concerned chiefly if not entirely with younger pupils, and whose work should lay a foundation on which more advanced study can be based. It aims also to make the reader think for himself. It is obviously far beyond the scope of the book, which is the fruit of over forty years' experience as teacher and examiner, to go into every detail of technical or other matters. The various individual points used for the illustration of basic principles have been selected merely to show the kind of procedure which can be followed, in the hope that the reader may himself work out similar procedures for other matters.

In some cases it may appear that I have mixed up the material of some chapters. For example, Chapter IV has some instruction on methods of practising which might seem to belong more properly to Chapter V. But one cannot put everything into entirely separate compartments and it seemed better to pursue a line of thought to its conclusion rather than to break off halfway through so as to conform strictly to chapter-headings.

In view of the fact that the title implies music teaching in general, it may be felt that there is too much of a preponderance of references to the piano. The reason is simple – the vast majority of teachers and students everywhere are concerned with that instrument. But the principles enunciated apply, *mutatis mutandis*, to any branch of music study, and non-pianists may well spend time working out their application to their own branches. I make no apology for a certain amount of repetitiveness. Some things cannot be stressed too often or too strongly; and many matters arise out of more than one context.

Finally, it may be suggested that I offer nothing but counsels of perfection. True – but what else is there to do? We may never achieve perfection but we must at least try to do so, otherwise we are not worthy to be called teachers.

II

The Teacher

It is not suggested that there is anything really new in the chapters which follow. The aim is to try to show application of common-sense methods in teaching. Students and teachers read many books on Psychology or on the Psychology of Teaching and the study of these is implied if not actually demanded by many current examination syllabuses. There is, of course, no objection at all to the study of such books; the trouble, as any experienced examiner knows, is that too often they are only half understood and the *practical* application of the principles they enunciate is not understood at all. To many people the terminology of Psychology is liable at times to be puzzling and explanations of that terminology almost equally so unless the writer is himself a born teacher who can see the difficulties through the students' eyes. It is not altogether easy for the average student to grasp the significance of such terms as Concept, Percept or Apperception. Even if he does, he may but rarely perceive their practical application in teaching. My own view is that the psychology of teaching is learnt by experience allied to common sense, and that books and examination questions are of value in proportion as they stress practical factors rather than theoretical abstractions.

The man to whom I, in common with many others, owe all that I am as a musician, teacher or otherwise, had never read a book on psychology applied to teaching in his life; had one suggested that he should do so his reaction would have been terse and quite probably unprintable. Yet he was without doubt the finest teacher anyone could wish to have, a man whose memory all his pupils without exception revere with deep gratitude and affection; a man who inspired us to attain heights of musicianship of which we would not have believed ourselves capable. But had one asked him the difference between a Concept and a Percept his reply would have been: 'No idea. What's it all about anyway? Get on and play your Bach!' He was what might be called an instinctive psychologist, applying in his teaching absolutely sound psychological principles which he had arrived at by the exercise of common sense and an inborn sympathy with, and understanding of, the student mind.

It is this sympathy and understanding that the teacher needs and must try to cultivate. Students are not machines, functioning automatically according to the laws of mechanics. Each is an individual human being; the mind, tastes and outlook of each differ from those of his fellows. So that although all have to learn the same fundamentals in whatever branch of music they are studying, the teacher's approach to and handling of each must be infinitely variable and adjustable. Some can grasp a new point with ease, others need lengthy and varied explanations; some can be allowed to exercise their own judgement to a fair extent, others need to be kept on a tighter rein. Two children may be of the same age yet one be far more mentally developed than the other. The possible comparisons are endless. But in every case sympathy and understanding by the teacher are essential.

It is hardly necessary to point out the importance of friendliness on the part of the teacher. Without it full co-operation from the pupil is unlikely, more especially in the case of children. A 'knuckle-rapping' attitude, whether literal or metaphorical, is to be deplored. The more personal liking the pupil has for the teacher, the more he will want to please him and the better he will work.

Young teachers need to realise that despite their own lack of years, to the child they may appear quite old. The difference between eight years and eighteen is far greater than that between twenty-eight and thirty-eight.

Equally, too, it must be remembered that not every child learns music willingly. For some parents the fact that little Tommy is learning the piano, or that little Mary achieved merit or honours in her last grade examination becomes a sort of status symbol; Tommy and Mary may be forced to learn whether or not they have any inclination or potentiality. Since this book is addressed to teachers rather than to parents, there is no need to expatiate on the foolishness, not to say iniquity, of driving the unwilling or unmusical child to learn, thereby probably killing any possibility of a liking for music which might otherwise develop; but the matter needs to be mentioned since it must affect the teacher's approach to and treatment of such children. If such a relationship can be established that the child looks forward to his weekly visit to the teacher, spending half an hour or so with someone he likes, then at least some progress is possible. Such cases need to be gently nursed along. Lessons must be as happy and easy-going as possible, dullness avoided.

With any young pupil (or any older one for that matter) humour, not merely good humour, is a great asset. Any little joke which will set the child giggling is all to the good and will help to bridge the gap between teacher and pupil. I may perhaps quote from my own experience here. Many years ago a girl of about eleven years, a rather 'old-fashioned' child, came for piano lessons and was sent away after her first lesson giggling over some silly remarks I had (deliberately) made. On arrival home her mother asked, 'How do you like Mr. Lovelock?' 'Oh, I like him; he has a sense of humour.' The right kind of contact had been made and although the child was not capable of more than average work, there was never any trouble in maintaining a happy relationship.

To say that the teacher's job is to teach is to state an obvious, even blatant truism. Nevertheless it must be said, since even in this age of text-books, refresher courses and so on there are still self-styled 'teachers' whose idea of teaching seems to be to let a pupil 'plough through' whatever work has been set, explaining nothing, demonstrating nothing and correcting little if anything. Such 'teachers' are luckily not numerous but any examiner knows that they exist – and suffers accordingly in the examination room.

The teacher himself needs, obviously, a thorough knowledge of his subject. He also needs humility and realisation that he can never know too much (or even, to be quite honest, enough), and that there is always something he can learn from somebody, even from pupils themselves. Too many teachers get stuck in a groove and either cannot get out of it or will not try to make the effort. They manage, perhaps, to evolve some kind of a method, and accumulate a limited teaching repertoire, and there they stick. No wondering whether perhaps their method may be capable of improvement and no attempt to incorporate new works into the repertoire. I recall a teacher telling me that: 'My pupil played such-and-such a group for her grade

V examination. I played it myself for the same exam forty years ago.' She had probably taught that same group for that same grade for the best part of forty years; and knowing the type I am quite prepared to believe that she never taught any other group. (One forbears to comment on a syllabus in which the same two pieces had remained for such a long period.) What can one say of such a stagnant outlook? It is not suggested that every new 'development in teaching method' is a good one (there are always plenty of 'crank' ideas in all branches of education), nor that every newly published set of teaching pieces is necessarily better than the longer-established ones. But new ideas of teaching and new material must be studied and their possible use at least considered.

Teaching repertoire should be as varied and comprehensive as possible so that material suitable for any individual pupil at any stage of development is always available. Some things, of course, will be permanently in the repertoire. Every piano student, for example, must sooner or later tackle some of Bach's 'Two-part Inventions'. In the case of advanced students the standard repertoire of such composers as Bach, Beethoven, Schumann, Chopin, Liszt, etc., must be studied. But in the more elementary stages the wider the repertoire and the more varied the use made of it the better. The really great works of the really great composers never lose their interest and attraction, but the more superficial 'easy teaching pieces' have not the same lasting power.

Some further reference to humility is desirable. As suggested above, there is always something that we can learn from somebody, however much we may know already. I recall a fellow-student who achieved a considerable reputation in opera. Despite her great gifts she would, even when at the height of her powers and reputation, continually return to her old teacher for coaching and advice. The renowned pianist, Paderewski, having achieved a European reputation, would still go back to Vienna for advice from his great teacher, Leschetizky.

As an examiner one meets all too often the work of the type of teacher who is far from competent. Examination results inevitably reflect this incompetence, but how often does the teacher ask himself who is really at fault, or realise that he himself is being examined through the work of his pupils? The tendency is to put the blame for poor results, even allowing for the variable ability of pupils, anywhere but where it really belongs. The pupils are lazy, they have been busy with school examinations, mother insisted on Mary taking the examination even though she was not ready, etc., etc. All these excuses may be valid enough in some cases, but they do not necessarily hold water. I recall visiting one big examination centre not long before starting this book and as soon as I arrived it was impressed on me that 'this is a bad time of the year for the children to have music examinations. They are tired and they've got their school exams' – and so on. The general standard of the work was depressing but most of the weaknesses were not due to the reasons put forward. Tiredness, school examinations, etc., may be responsible for lack of absolutely complete preparation, for the odd slips which would have been eradicated by a little longer practice. But they are no excuse at all for *fundamental* faults in the work. If the examiner has a batch of candidates from one teacher all of whom, say, sit too close to the keyboard, or whose finger-work is stiff, or who hold the violin wrongly, or whose breathing (in singing) is noisy, he cannot accept tiredness, etc., as an excuse.   There is something wrong with the teach-ing method itself.

The solution is really quite simple, if the teacher concerned has the humility to perceive it.   Put your pride in your pocket, go to a teacher who you know gets consistently good results and get his advice and assis-tance.   Admitted that it is not altogether easy to step down from one's self-created pedestal, to admit that one is oneself at fault.   But it is the only way.

III

Basic Principles

THREE fundamental facts must be clearly understood:
  1 All that we learn is ultimately based on memory.
  2 All that we learn is cumulative.
  3 All that we learn must be based on understanding.
  To the experienced teacher these statements may appear obvious, but it is an unfortunate fact that their importance is often not realised if, indeed, they are considered at all.   The would-be teacher who does not understand these fundamentals and who does not pass on an appreciation of them, directly or indirectly, to his pupils, is to a large extent working in the dark; results will inevitably be 'hit or miss'.   Further, they apply whatever subject is being studied and whether it be practical or theoretical.

1.   Leaving aside the development of musicianship, the aim of teaching should be the formation of correct habits.   A habit is an action which has become automatic, *i.e.* virtually a motor action like that of the limbs in walking.   But before this stage is reached, the movements have first to be mastered under conscious control: to put it quite simply, we have deliberately to think what we are doing.   By continual, thoughtful and accurate repetition the muscles concerned can be safely trusted to work on their own, leaving the conscious mind free to attend to other matters.   The action has been memorised.

  To fix the correct performance of the action in the

memory, repetition is essential. Each repetition, provided it is correctly done, deepens the impression, but it is obviously impossible to lay down any rule as to the number of repetitions that may be needed in any given instance. This will depend on (*a*) the mentality of the pupil and (*b*) the difficulty or complexity of the action. (See Chapter V, Lessons and Practice.)

The principles of memory and repetition apply in everything that we learn, whether it involves a physical action or not. The young child at school learns his 'tables' – twice two are four, twice three are six and so on – purely by rote. And although rote-learning is sometimes decried, a certain amount of it is essential. In due course, and after ample repetition, he 'knows' that, for example, three threes are nine and three sixes are eighteen; so that if told to multiply 63 by 3 he does not need to work through the three-times table step by step from 'three ones are three' to reach the answer of 189. The correct result of each of the two multiplications involved comes to his conscious mind immediately. Unless the elementary 'tables' are firmly fixed in the memory he will never get very far with arithmetic.

A similar process applies in learning to write, which does involve the performance of physical actions. The first step is the formation of individual letters, each of which has to be shaped with conscious thought as to the directions in which the pen must move. By the time the pupil has traced a sufficient number of 'a's' (the number of course varying with the individual) he will no longer need to think consciously of the movements required. A habit will have been formed and the letter will, as it were, write itself. The building of letters into words follows a similar process. The reader may care to write, the two words 'Dear Sir'. He will not find it necessary to think of seven separate letters –

D–E–A–R–S–I–R; his pen will trace automatically the two composite symbols 'dear' and 'sir' without any conscious effort to form the letters or to spell the words.

Exactly similar processes apply in learning music, whether practical or theoretical. The piano student has first to learn the correct position of fingers and hand and arm, and must learn it so thoroughly that whenever he puts his fingers on the keys they and the hand and the arm automatically assume this correct position. The teacher must first explain and demonstrate and the pupil must imitate, faults being corrected if they occur. Repetition must be ample – hands on keys – hands on lap – until no fault occurs and it is evident that the pupil has really grasped the idea, *i.e.* is memorising the correct position. The work must be continued at home and if done properly the whole thing should be mastered by the next lesson, fingers, hand and arm assuming the correct position automatically.

It must be stressed that the frequency with which an impression is renewed is of the greatest importance. It is not just a matter of doing the same thing an indefinite number of times at one sitting – too much continuous repetition induces tiredness and boredom. The essential is to have as many 'sittings' as possible every day, even though they will only be short ones. The pupil should be told that every time he passes his piano, even if just *en route* from one room to another, he should sit down at the instrument, put fingers on the keys correctly, drop to lap, repeat four or five times, and then go on to whatever else he intended to do. If he passes the piano ten times in a day then he should have ten 'sittings'. Experience proves that this method works and with a reasonably intelligent pupil it works with surprising speed, always providing that the proper foundation has been laid at the lesson.

Such a matter as holding the violin correctly should be dealt with on similar lines. Pick up the instrument, get it and the hand and arm in proper position; put it down, pick it up again, and so on, always with the most careful thought.

As to the correction of faults it may be worth while recalling an examination experience. My colleague was questioning a candidate for a violin teacher's diploma and the candidate had stressed the importance of keeping the elbow well under the instrument. The examiner asked, 'And what would you do if the pupil just won't keep his elbow under?' Like a flash came the reply, 'Keep on telling him!' – to my own amusement and somewhat to my colleague's discomfiture. The answer was, of course, the only correct one. Having explained and demonstrated, the only thing to do is to 'keep on telling him'. This is all the more necessary when the correct action (or position as in the above case) presents some degree of difficulty. Unceasing watchfulness is essential.

The part which memory plays in theoretical study should be obvious. 'Rules' must be memorised before they can be properly observed so that their correct application may become automatic. A great deal of poor written work is due to the fact that the student does not really study (and hence fix in the memory) the text of the book being used. It is not a matter of literally memorising every word, but of grasping, understanding and retaining in the mind the *substance* of the text. (Actually, one has met examination candidates, especially in India, who appear to have memorised every single word of a text-book so that a question on, say, some point of teaching will be answered by a literal quotation of something the examiner may have written himself. But in such cases it generally seems to happen that a request to rephrase the answer so that it could be understood by a small child is met with a blank stare, and further questioning may reveal a complete lack of understanding of the meaning or application of the passage so fluently quoted, together with a complete inability to demonstrate on the instrument. This kind of thing is rote-learning at its worst.)

The lack of real study, as opposed to mere reading through, is sometimes indirectly the fault of the teacher who does not impress on the pupil the right way to set about things. The instruction 'go ahead with the next chapter' is not enough unless the pupil already understands what is required of him and what 'going ahead' should really mean. Concentrated *study* is needed, with careful comparison and collation of text with examples; and rote-learning of essentials must not be despised. For example, the difference between a major triad and a minor one must be learned by rote, visually as well as aurally, as must also the kind of triad which occurs on each degree of a scale. In elementary harmony, at least, the treatment of certain chord-progressions needs to be learned by rote and memorised, as, for example, the normal movement of the upper parts in the progression IVa – Va – 'top three parts in contrary motion to the bass, each moving to the nearest available note'; or in Va – VIa – 'double the 3rd of VI, approaching it by steps in contrary motion'. (Admitted that there are other possibilities in both cases, but the beginner has to learn to walk before he can run.) If such points as these are memorised, with ample practice in working examples (and equally ample demonstration by the teacher) accurate writing of such progressions will sooner or later become automatic.

Here again, 'keep on telling him' applies, as well as 'keep on showing him'. It may be mentioned, too, that however detailed may be the instruction given in the text-book and however simply and clearly it may be expressed, there are but few students who can manage without at least some step-by-step demonstration by the teacher. Five minutes with pencil and manuscript paper, building up an example note by note, chord by chord and explaining each step as it is taken are worth an hour's reading by the student. This, though many teachers of 'theory' appear not to realise it, applies from the most elementary to the most advanced stages of work. If the teacher really knows his job, the pupil can learn more from following the harmonisation of an eight-bar melody at his lesson, the teacher explaining in detail the reason for everything that he does, than by reading every book that has ever been written on the subject. The old saying that example is better than precept still holds good. (There is also the purely economic aspect that if the writer of the harmony text book were to include all the detail that he may introduce into a personal lesson, nobody would be able to afford to buy the book!)

The function of memory in aural training is all too often overlooked. Even absolute (or perfect) pitch is merely one aspect of memory – memorised pitch. One presumes that in theory it could be 'taught', but to those who possess it, it seems to have come without conscious cultivation; they 'have always had it'. The memory appears to be particularly highly and early developed in this direction and no deliberate effort is made. (I myself cannot remember not having absolute pitch since my first music lessons at the age of six.) It is not, by the way, altogether an unmixed blessing, however useful for examination aural tests. Having to perform on an instrument which is even slightly above or below the pitch to which one is used can put one badly off one's stride.   Brass bands, who still adhere to the old 'high pitch', are a source of irritation since a piece which one knows to be in, say, F major sounds nearer to F sharp.   More worrying still is the fact that with increasing age and due presumably to some deterioration in the mechanism of the ear, one hears things a semitone sharp.   It is distinctly bothersome to hear Beethoven's Fifth Symphony in C *sharp* minor!

To revert, however, to aural training as such.   The fact that one can recognise a major 3rd, or a minor triad, or anything else, as such is due to the fact that one has consciously or unconsciously memorised their sound effect, and aural training must be based on an appreciation of this, coupled with the necessity of repetition to fix the effect in the memory.   (See Chapter VII – Aural Work.)

Finally with regard to the memory as a basis of learning we must refer to performance from memory. In passing it may be mentioned that most singers, even quite elementary students, learn to dispense with the printed copy; indeed it is generally expected of them. Yet instrumentalists below diploma standard rarely do so.   Playing from memory, as far as the average pupil is concerned, is looked upon as something of an accomplishment, hardly to be expected of ordinary mortals. What such a pupil (or his teacher) fails to realise is that the fact that after a week's practice he can play a piece more fluently than when he first read it means that he has at least partly memorised it.   Admitted that in some cases complete memorisation is such a slow and laboured process that the attempt is hardly worth the effort; but much more could be achieved if it were only realised that in learning anything one is memorising all the time and if there were greater confidence in the ability to memorise.   The pupil who says, 'I can't memorise', obviously never will memorise. If he makes up his mind that he can then he is at least half-way to doing so.

*   *   *

2. The close connection between memory and the cumulative aspect of learning should be obvious; it is the cumulative aspect itself which is apt to be under-estimated. Every new fact that is learnt is at least to some extent derived from or based on what has already been mastered; every new point of technique depends in some way or other on what has already been achieved. But if the previous knowledge or achievement is not soundly based, then the new work cannot be undertaken successfully. This obviously means that there must be no weakness at all in the ultimate, most elementary basis, otherwise the superstructure may eventually collapse. No building can stand if its foundations are not secure.

No progress is possible on the piano, for example, unless the correct position of fingers, hands and arms, and their correct muscular condition (see Relaxation, page 70) have been mastered and an unbreakable habit has been formed. Five-finger exercises must be built on a foundation of two- and three-finger exercises for *legato* and good finger action, and for these a correct hand position is a prerequisite. Scales cannot be attempted until simple five-finger exercises can be done properly. Correct fingering of scales in the octave position must be automatic before 3rds or 6ths can be safely tackled. And so on, indefinitely. Similarly with paper work. Understanding of intervals depends on understanding of the structure of the major scale and a safe know-ledge of major key-signatures; even elementary har-mony is a hopeless task unless intervals are not only understood but instantaneously recognisable.

And similarly with aural work. I have sometimes been asked for an infallible method of recognising the key to which a passage modulates, as if this particular type of test could be isolated. It cannot. The ear must be trained from the most elementary stages – recognition of scale-degrees, recognition of intervals, recognition of triads and so on.

From all this it is obvious that periodical revision of previous work is essential. Especially in paper work students have a tendency to let any given matter fade from the mind once they have 'studied the chapter and worked the exercises', and but rarely think of doing any revision, or re-reading of earlier work. It is the teacher's job to ensure that this is done.

A warning may here be given of the necessity of really finding out what a new pupil does or does not know. It is not enough, for example, to accept the pupil's assurance that he knows all about intervals. He must be questioned practically. 'What is an augmented 4th above D? What is the inversion of a diminished 3rd', and so on *ad lib*. Unless the answers are instantaneous and correct, intervals should be re-studied. Even quite advanced students may suddenly reveal strange gaps in their elementary knowledge, gaps which may lead to serious weaknesses in the work they are doing. I remember the shock of discovering that a pupil working for the degree of Bachelor of Music, work involving quite advanced harmony and counterpoint, could not recognise an augmented 4th when she saw one. I willingly admit that this was a salutary lesson for me, her teacher.

The whole matter of cumulation may briefly be summed up thus:

(*a*) Ensure an absolutely solid foundation.
(*b*) Build on this step by step, logically.

(c) Relate each step to the preceding one.

(d) Revise frequently.

*   *   *

3. As already stated, a certain amount of learning by rote, whatever the subject or branch of it, is essential. But everything must be done to ensure that the pupil understands (a) what has to be done, (b) exactly how to do it and (c), at least as far as his mental development permits, why.

(a) Presents no difficulty; a mere matter of instruction by the teacher.

(b) Is again a matter of instruction, by explanation and demonstration, but great care is needed to ensure that the method of working is clearly grasped. This involves not only explanation and demonstration but also practice by the pupil during the lesson. The point, whether theoretical or practical, must be worked at with varying approaches and explanations until it is clear that it is fully grasped and understood. Only then can the pupil be left to work at it on his own. Explanation without demonstration is useless; but the important thing is for the pupil himself to tackle the problem under the teacher's eye.

(c) The younger and less mentally developed the pupil, the more he has to take on trust. Nevertheless, some explanation of the reason for any given procedure is desirable. The essential point is that any explanation, whether of the 'how' or the 'why' or of anything else must be made in language simple enough to be understood. This is another blatantly obvious statement, but is necessary in view of the way in which examination candidates are liable to answer questions, whether verbally or in writing. The question, for example, may deal with the difference between weight touch and energy touch at the piano and may ask for an explanation aimed at a child of ten years. All too often the answer is phrased in terms which would puzzle anybody who had not an understanding of the anatomy of the hand and arm. Alternatively it may be badly muddled and equally badly expressed owing to incomplete understanding of what has been read in some book on technique. (High-powered technical jargon is a cause of much puzzlement and misunderstanding.) Not long before I started writing this book I was questioning a diploma candidate on *cantabile* touch and was told that the key must be depressed 'gradually'. Whether this statement is valid or, indeed, whether it has any meaning at all is arguable in any case, but it was quite obvious that the candidate was merely trying to quote what she had read, without any proper comprehension. A request for a demonstration of a 'gradual' depression of the key produced results which could only be called ludicrous.

One of the first things that any teacher has to learn is to see things through the mind of the pupil and to allow always for his age, stage of mental development and limited background and knowledge. Because the older person can grasp a point with ease, it does not follow that the child can do the same. Far from it. His vocabulary, for one thing, is undeveloped, so that terminology which would be understood by an adult may mean nothing to him. Even with the adult pupil it is far better to use the most elementary terminology, since musically speaking he may be little if anything above the level of the child.

Such a word as 'relaxation' (of which the real significance in piano playing is misunderstood by so many teachers and students) is quite above the head of the average child. Yet to get some examination candidates to use the simple word 'looseness' is rather like trying to get blood out of a stone! To tell a child to 'relax the weight of the arm into the key' is simply idiotic. Why not say 'drop'? Matters are sometimes complicated by the unwillingness of many pupils to admit that they do not understand – fear, conscious or otherwise, of being thought dull and unintelligent. Any budding teacher studying a book on teaching should be continually asking himself (a) do I really understand this sentence myself? and (b) how could I make it clear to a child? Any text-book must assume some background knowledge on the part of the reader. A harmony book assumes knowledge of Rudiments; a book on psychology assumes a knowledge of the language in which it is written sufficient to enable the reader to understand the meanings of the terms used. But the elementary student lacks background, which the teacher must provide in a manner intelligible at the student's stage of development.

The use of analogy and of association of ideas is vitally important. In connection with time in music, text-books refer to 'regular pulsation'. How many children of, say, eight years know (a) the meaning of 'pulsation' or (b) the exact significance of 'regular' in this connection? Yet it is easily made clear to the youngest child if one speaks of an 'even beat' – 'pom-pom-pom' – with the analogy of the ticking of a clock. 'You know how a clock ticks. It just goes on and on quite evenly, tick-tock-tick-tock. Now, you are a clock. Let's hear you tick.' Dealt with like this, comprehension and understanding are easy and certain.

An easy colloquial manner of speech in teaching is desirable. Even nonsense syllables have their uses (and incidentally help the child to realise that the teacher is a normal human being). Such a rhythmic figure as that involved in 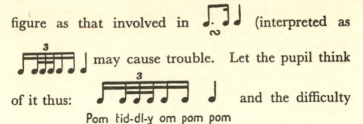 (interpreted as

may cause trouble. Let the pupil think

of it thus: and the difficulty

Pom tid-dl-y om pom pom

vanishes.

Lack of clear understanding may be due to *incomplete* explanation. The teacher continually hammers home 'count evenly' but does not make sufficiently clear exactly what is to be counted evenly. Count the *beats* evenly and make sure that subdivisions are correctly placed between these even counts. Consider this little exercise in counting:

Ex. 1

1 2 3 4 & 1 2 3 4 8 1 & 2 & 3 4 & 1 2 3 4

Any examiner knows that sooner or later a candidate will present it like this:

Ex. 2

1 2 3 4 8 1 2 3 4 8 1 & 2 & 3 4 & 1 2 3 4

The candidate is certainly 'counting evenly' but he is making the beat subdivisions the same length as the beats themselves. This is due to not understanding that the *beats*, *i.e.* the numbers 1, 2, 3, 4, must be even. Experience in the examination room suggests that often the fault lies actually with the teacher, who apparently does not himself realise that the rhythm is wrong. Incidentally there is no guarantee that the use of French time-names will produce any better result.

Consider, again, the matter of the relative lengths of notes, which would be better called the relative lengths of sounds. The pupil learns by rote (as he must) that two minims make a semibreve, two crotchets make a minim, and so on, but this does not guarantee accurate time-keeping. Far from it. What is so rarely made clear is that the length of a sound means the number of beats, or the fraction of a beat which it lasts. If the beats are crotchets, then a minim must be held while we count two beats – 1, 2 or 2, 3 or 3, 4 as the case may be. And these beats must be counted perfectly evenly.

It is not to be assumed that the advice given in this chapter is necessarily and automatically productive of first-class results. However well the teacher may understand his job, however careful and painstaking he may be, in the end results depend on the intelligence of the pupil. One cannot make bricks without straw. Nevertheless, even the dullest pupil can be led some way along the road if the teacher is willing to work on the right lines and to exercise sympathy and tact.

IV

Method

THERE is a certain amount of truth in the old saying
that any method is better than none at all, but the
teacher should not be satisfied with just 'any' method.
What is needed is one which is based on logical
principles and logical development and which will
produce results which are musically good enough to
justify it.

The approach to any individual pupil must be variable according to his character and mentality and the
approach to any given matter being studied must be
similarly variable. But whatever the type of pupil,
whatever his particular cast of mind, the basic essentials
must be mastered and a proper foundation laid. The
method must be there.

In any method and in any subject or branch of it,
it is essential to take first things first – another glimpse
of the obvious which is often overlooked. If an
examiner has ten diploma candidates and asks each one
what ground he would try to cover at the first lesson
with a previously untaught piano pupil, it is a safe bet
that not more than two of them will mention posture,
hand position and muscular freedom. (This, as I myself know only too well, is not an exaggeration.) There
will be plenty of talk of showing the pupil the inside of
the piano, testing his ear, teaching him the notes on
both keyboard and paper and 'giving him exercises' –
though exactly what exercises is rarely specified and if

they are, then they are pretty sure to be quite unsuit-able! But of the one thing which must be mastered as soon as possible, no mention at all.

Although the correct hand position at the piano is perfectly natural (though one has met candidates who insist that it is not) it nevertheless has to be taught, and taught in such a way that correctness becomes a habit (see page 37). If this is not done *at once* faults are almost certain to arise and will need to be put right. This involves the thoroughly bad process of *unlearning*.

With a stringed instrument the first things are correct posture and holding of the instrument and the bow.

It may be suggested that it is equally important to deal straight away with aural work or notation or the names of the keys of the piano. True enough. But the purely physical should come first since it involves the building up of correct physical habits. Aural work, essential though it is, is not liable to involve unlearning, while notation and the names of the keys are matters of rote-learning.

In passing one may mention a strange reluctance on the part of some examination candidates to put first things first in connection with teaching the notes either on paper or on the keyboard. The one thing so rarely mentioned is that first of all the pupil must learn the musical alphabet.

With a properly taught student the need for un-learning should never arise; correct building on a proper foundation obviates it. Unfortunately, as any good teacher knows, it is a necessity which continually occurs with previously badly taught pupils. How often does one have to rectify bad hand and finger position, muscular stiffness, wrong holding of the violin or bow, erroneous ideas on time... the list could be extended indefinitely.

When the need for unlearning does arise, especially with purely physical matters, the only way is to go right down to bedrock and start again from the beginning; and to forbid the pupil to play or sing whatever may have been learned under wrong methods. (The latter is not easy to ensure and one has to trust to the pupil's desire to improve and his faith in his new teacher.) In other words, do not try to patch up the holes, but rather scrap the old garment completely and make a new one. This comprehensive process obviously will not be needed if the fault or faults are relatively minor ones, or relatively slight; in such cases patching-up may often be managed satisfactorily. But with deep-seated faults the only thing is to go right back to the beginning. If a lawn has only a few small patches of weed they may easily be dealt with. But if it is simply nothing but weed, no lawn at all, the only cure is to dig the whole thing up and re-sow.

It must be understood that most if not all faults are basically due to wrong thinking, or simply to not thinking at all. A bad hand position will arise because the student is not thinking correctly, or possibly because he has never been taught to think correctly on this matter. Wrong fingering may be due simply to not thinking – the student just 'does not bother about it'. One of the first things the pupil has to learn is that he must always concentrate his attention, in other words he must 'think what he is doing', and the teacher must aim to build up this attitude of mind. It is not just a matter of not letting the mind wander (and how troublesome some small children can be in this respect!), but of keeping the attention firmly fixed on the matter in hand, knowing what has to be done and how to do it, and striving to do it correctly.

In his book *The Science of Pianoforte Technique** (one of the best books ever written on the subject) Thomas Fielden states categorically that, 'it must be realised that technique is mainly mental'. This does not imply that muscular development is unnecessary, far from it; it means that every action must be under proper mental control – 'mind over matter'. The control is at first conscious, gradually becoming unconscious. This obviously postulates right thinking from the start and right thinking is impossible without clear understanding of the 'how' and the 'why'.

On the piano, two of the commonest and most deep-seated faults are lack of relaxation and wrong position of hand and arm. We will deal with these in some detail so as to exemplify the kind of procedure which may be followed.

Lack of relaxation, *i.e.* stiffness, arises from two causes, mental and physical. The former is due to wrong thinking, the student not understanding what is needed and why. The latter is due to lack of actual exercise of fingers, wrists, etc., rather like the stiffness of a door-hinge which needs oiling.

Apart from not having been instructed in the undesirability (to put it no stronger) of stiffness, many students fall into it because they have no idea of the physical sensation of having hands, arms, etc., relaxed. To put it more simply, they do not know *what it feels like*.

This matter of 'what it feels like' is of the utmost importance. The physical sensation or feeling of an action or a condition or a position must be consciously realised and memorised, and reproduced until it becomes a habit. It is no use telling the pupil to 'keep loose' unless and until he knows what it feels like to be loose. To break down stiffness which has

* Macmillan.

become ingrained it is necessary to get right down to something basic, something so simple that he can hardly go wrong, and then build on it. Also it may be necessary to go to extremes, to swing the pendulum, as it were, right over to the other side. (The result of this, in the case of relaxation, may be that for a while the pupil will feel that he has no control of the keys at all. He need not worry – the control will come.) Tell the pupil to imagine that he has come home completely tired out and let him 'flop out' in an armchair, quite flabby all over. Tell him to think, deliberately, what he feels like – utterly relaxed. This is certainly going to extremes but is often necessary.

Next, seated at the piano, let him drop his arms by his sides reproducing the same relaxed feeling. Now raise the forearms, placing the fingers on the keys, still with the same feeling. Drop the arms by the sides again, then raise and place fingers on the keys, repeating this several times always with full attention to reproducing the relaxed sensation. By now the idea should have begun to take root and a week's practice with several sittings daily should consolidate the position pretty safely. Continual vigilance is needed, naturally, to ensure that there is no slipping back into the former wrong method.

Wrong position of hands, etc., is generally due to wrong thinking which stems from bad teaching, though it may be due to a physical weakness. It is first necessary to see that the seat is the correct height. There are varying schools of thought about this, some advocating a low seat, some a high one and some an intermediate position. The fact of the matter is that height of seat must vary according to the physical build of the individual and should be such as to put arms and wrists in a natural and easy position. (To obtain the proper level of forearm and wrist a long-armed person generally needs a higher seat than a short-armed one.) The forearm should be approximately horizontal, the upper arm sloping slightly forward. Sitting too close to the keyboard, with the elbow at a right angle, tends to lower the wrist and to induce stiffness in the upper arm. Too low a seat causes a dropped wrist and impedes agility; too high a seat, with sloping forearm and over-high wrist, certainly facilitates double octaves but militates against a good *cantabile*.

The seat being at the right height, correct shape of hands and fingers is a simple matter. If the arm hangs loosely by the side the hand (relaxed) falls naturally into the proper shape, with the fingers easily curved. *Keeping this feeling*, and without any alteration in the shape of the hand, raise the forearm and place the fingers on the keys in the five-finger position. The job is done. As usual, repeat the process until i t becomes automatic.

It is a rather strange fact that some pupils find difficulty in keeping the curved shape of the fingers on the keys even though, as has been shown, it is perfectly natural. The solution, as may be expected, is to 'keep on telling him', and to watch as he depresses each key.

It should be obvious that the correction of stiffness and of incorrect position can and should be done simultaneously. To aim for relaxation while permitting a bad position, or *vice versa*, is poor teaching.

With regard to bad hand position due to a physical weakness, we may instance the type of hand where the knuckles are double-jointed and tend continually to fall in. 'Going the whole hog' is needed here. Get things right at the lesson and allow the pupil to do *nothing at all*, but 'hands on keys, hands on lap' for a whole week – longer if necessary. If he really uses his intelligence the problem will soon be solved.

This matter of 'going the whole hog' needs some further discussion. A well-tried axiom of teaching is 'Teach one thing at a time', and although in normal circumstances it need not be taken absolutely literally, there are times when it must be. It might be better expressed as, 'Teach one step of one thing at a time.' The beginner, for example, need not be taught *only* hand position at his first lesson (or only how to hold the violin); a start should also be made on, say, aural work and note-identification at the keyboard. The various matters are at this stage in quite separate compartments. If some physical fault is really deep-seated, however, the quickest way is to concentrate on its cure to the temporary exclusion of everything else. This may seem drastic but it works and works speedily, provided the co-operation of the pupil is obtained by a clear explanation of its necessity.

Reverting to 'what it feels like', two further examples may be helpful.

(i) Singers have a common fault of gasping – noisy in-breathing (a disease which also seems to afflict some radio announcers and numerous American film-stars!). It is due, of course, to constriction of the throat, impeding the inward passage of the air. The throat needs to be loosely open. A way of achieving this is to open the mouth with a loosely dropped lower jaw and remain quite still *feeling* the relaxed sensation in the throat. Now deliberately tense the throat so as to appreciate the different feeling. Relax again and inhale gently, concentrating on keeping the relaxed sensation. Practice on these lines should ultimately cure the fault.

(ii) Out-of-tune playing on a stringed instrument is due to the finger not being on exactly the right spot on the string. Suppose that the fourth finger notes are persistently flat. Physically this means that the finger is not sufficiently separated from its neighbour the third. Move it until the note is properly in tune and concentrate on this 'wider' feeling in some such exercise as:

Ex.3

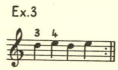

starting very slowly and gradually speeding up.

It may be noted that the above paragraphs furnish further examples of the function of memory (Chapter III) – memory in these cases of 'what it feels like'.

Mention above of 'something basic' leads to a consideration of the importance of *basic physical actions*. Too often a pupil may find difficulty with some new point of technique because he does not understand the quite simple action which lies at the root of it. Some practical examples will make the principle clear.

(i) Weight touch at the piano depends on the simple mechanical principle that any weight when released will fall and the pupil has to be taught to apply this fact in his approach to the key. (It may be worth mentioning that youngsters do not necessarily realise that the hands and arms do possess weight.) The basic action, therefore, is to hold up the hands and arms and then let them drop freely on to the lap. This, of course, is an exaggeration of what one will ultimately do at the keyboard, but it is a sure method of teaching the essential action and ensures appreciation of 'what it feels like'. The next step is to drop, from a few inches, on the side of the hand on to black keys (say E flat and G flat); then on to the middle finger with the hand in the proper playing position, making sure that the wrist relaxes, (*i.e.* 'flops') immediately the keybed is reached. Next proceed to some such exercise as this:

Ex. 4

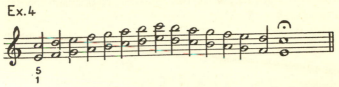

with left hand an octave lower, gradually diminishing the size of the drop (but concentrating on keeping the *feeling* of 'drop'), until it can be done with the fingers starting in actual contact with the key-surface – each note being 'prepared'. One point needs watching at every stage: there must be no attempt to stop the drop as it were when the keybed is reached, otherwise the tone will be poor, lacking body. The pupil must imagine that his hands are going to drop *right through the keys*. Compare the follow-through in a stroke at tennis. To get the ball back across the net one does not so much aim 'at' it as 'through' it. The finger is the racquet, the tone is the ball; aim through it. Ex. 4, or whatever comparable exercise is used, must, of course, be prac-tised with varied weight behind the drop, light, medium and heavy.

(ii) The difficulty of *legato* pedalling, which is apt to bother many students at first, is due to not realising that at the point of change the hand and foot move in contrary motion, foot coming up as hand goes down. It is this basic action which must first be mastered and it is really quite a simple matter. Hold the forearm horizontal, away from the keyboard and place the right foot flat on the floor. Practise dropping the hand from the wrist and simultaneously raising the foot from the ankle-joint, realising clearly that *they move in opposite directions*. Do the same letting the whole forearm, not only the hand, drop a little. All this will fix in the mind the 'contrary-motion feeling'. At the keyboard a rhythmic approach is essential in steps such as the following:

Ex. 5

It is important to feel the accent on the upward movement of the foot – UP-down.

(iii) As a final example consider such a passage as the following from Grieg's 'Wedding Day':

Ex. 6

The basic action here is a quick alternation of the hands and there must be a clear realisation that the accents come in the left hand which is normally the weaker member. Begin by patting the knees with alternate hands, left, right, left, right, feeling groups of four with accents in the left hand and avoiding muscular stiffness. Most people can do this for quite a long time

at a stretch with but little trouble. Next practice
exercises like this:

Ex.7

starting slowly and gradually speeding up. Then in
some kind of alternating chords:

Ex.8

The Grieg should now present but little difficulty
provided (*a*) muscular stiffness is avoided and (*b*) the
left-hand accents are held firmly in the mind ('Whack
them out in your head').

An important digression may be made here, arising
from mention of the left hand as being normally the
weaker member. Unless great care is taken the right
hand will always tend to 'grab' an undue amount of the
player's attention so that the left hand may be more or
less left to look after itself. This weakness comes
especially to the fore in passages where the two hands
are on equal terms, such as scales, arpeggios and chords.
In running passages the left hand may lose its grip on
the rhythm and in chords its tone may not properly
balance that of the right hand. The self-evident

solution is deliberately to focus the attention more on the left hand than on the right and to *listen* more carefully. In other words, *think about it*.

The matter of 'what it feels like' brings us to a fuller consideration of the purely physical aspect of performance. Reduced to its lowest terms and disregarding the purely musical side entirely, any performance involves a certain series of physical actions done in a certain definite order; and, again in lowest terms, we have to learn what these actions are and the order in which they must occur. In other words, we must know not only the notes to be played or sung but the physical actions needed to produce these notes correctly. It is not for a moment suggested that our conscious thinking must be exclusively on these lines but in the actual process of learning it must be to some extent. As the learner progresses from the initial stages he will, if he is properly taught, be continually storing up in his mind facts and series of actions which are as it were filed for future reference and which can be drawn on when appropriate.

As an example, the well-trained piano student will have mastered the elementary rule 'next-door notes, next-door fingers; next-door-but-one notes, next-door-but-one fingers'* and will apply it automatically. So that if he reads such a passage as:

Ex.9

he should finger it correctly as 1, 3, 2, 4, 3, 5, 4, 2 without any conscious thought and will not need any fingering marked. (Incidentally, many teachers fail to

* But, alas, how many have never even heard of it!

realise that editorial fingering is largely based on the rule given above and that the rule itself derives from the natural fall of the hand into the five-finger position.)

The necessity of 'thinking physically' is apt to arise in the correction of wrong notes. Broadly speaking, wrong notes on the piano are due to:

(*a*) misreading;

(*b*) wrong fingering;

(*c*) hand too wide open;

(*d*) hand not open enough.

(This does not cover the matter completely but will serve for our present purpose.)

(*a*) See Chapter V.

(*b*) Wrong fingering is mostly a matter of careless reading (see below) but also may be due to wrong or careless thinking. Consider the following from a Czerny study:

Ex.10

The first bar establishes the finger pattern 1, 3, 2, 4, 3, 5 and the second bar begins with 1, 3, 2. The result is that instead of playing G with the third finger at * the pupil plays A with the fourth. He has failed to note that the pattern has changed. It is very little use for the teacher to say, 'don't play A, play G'. The proper comment is 'third finger not fourth'. In other words, think of the finger which plays the note rather than of the name of the note. If A with the fourth finger is played instead of G with the third, the correct series of physical actions is broken.

Thinking of the finger rather than of the note is especially important in part-playing on the piano. Long notes with a moving part against them in the same hand are a continual source of trouble. In such a passage as the following:

Ex. 11

the problem is to ensure the sustaining of the minim F with the fourth finger and the D with the thumb. To say 'Hold the F, hold the D' is not enough. It must be 'Hold the fourth, hold the thumb' – remembering, of course, that 'holding' does not mean pressing down on the key-bed, but leaving just enough weight in the key to keep it depressed.

(*c*) and (*d*) These involve the kind of adjustment referred to above in connection with out-of-tuneness on a stringed instrument. In the following:

Ex. 12

a small hand may miss the top C and the fifth finger either strike B or 'splash' B and C together. The hand is not sufficiently open, the gap between third and fifth is too small. Here again, it is useless to say 'C not B'. The pupil must be told to open the hand more on its fifth finger side. Conversely, with such a passage

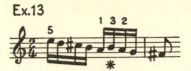

Ex.13

the third finger at * may strike C instead of B.   'Close up your hand (and remember what it feels like').

In passing it may be mentioned that extensions need special care and thought.   This kind of thing:

Ex.14

is liable to produce a crop of wrong notes with the thumb.   Practise, *slowly*, in sections as marked by the brackets, concentrating on the feel of the 9th stretch, in every case opening the hand as far as it will go without stiffening.

The above passage (which is further dealt with in chapter V) gives rise to two more important comments.

(i) There is an invariable tendency to 'squirt' at the top of each upward run so that as here the effect is rather like:

Ex.15

Superficially this would appear to be due to the natural weakness of the fourth and fifth fingers and this certainly has something to do with it.   But the real reason is lack of rhythmic control – a matter of right thinking.

The tendency is to think in groups of eight semi-quavers:

i.e. thinking *from* the accents instead of *to* them. The pupil must learn to 'think forward', to 'think round the corner'. To achieve this, practise thus:

When in strict time again, concentrate on the two notes before the leap and the one which follows it. Nonsense syllables help:

Thinking forward, *to* the accent, is always essential.

(ii) A more purely physical point also arises. For the 9th stretch the hand must be extended, but for the next note, the second semiquaver of the group, it must be closed up to the five-finger position. There is thus a double adjustment to be made at high speed and this must be consciously realised – open, shut, open, shut. Here again the inexperienced teacher may say for the second note of the second scale 'C not D' where he should say 'Close your hand'.

Reference was made above to change of pattern in connection with Ex. 10. This, especially in studies, is a frequent source of trouble since the pupil is not prepared in advance for the necessary physical adjustments.

Note the importance of being 'prepared in advance', whether for change of pattern or for anything else. Much stumbling over tricky passages will be avoided if the pupil has fixed in his mind where such passages occur and is ready for them. Forewarned is forearmed. If it is felt necessary to pencil-mark a regular trouble spot, it is not particularly helpful just to put a ring round it. Far better to put an arrow pointing towards it, in the preceding bar. The one thing which must be avoided is 'funk' on the part of the pupil. He knows that a tricky patch is coming and his reaction may be 'I know I'm going to make a mess of it' – and consequently he *will* make a mess of it. It must be impressed on him that as long as he is ready for it he can do it correctly, taking it in his stride. Concentrate, be prepared, but do not get worried.

With regard to pattern and adjustments, consider another quotation from Czerny:

Ex.19

| *a* | and | *b* | in isolation present no trouble at all; they both lie easily under the fingers. The snag is the adjustment needed at | *c* |; the hand has to open out suddenly for the second finger to reach its B. Mental preparation from the beginning of this bar is essential.

4

A possibly still more troublesome instance is shown in the following:

Ex.20

The first two bars are simple and if the pupil cannot manage them at sight he should go back and learn the scale of E major!   Bar 3, although the pattern changes, lies comfortably under the slightly extended hand.   In bar 4, however, arm movement up and down the keyboard is suddenly demanded, and it is not gradual as in bars 1 and 2, but swift, and with an arpeggio which is far less simple than the opening scale passage.   The pupil must realise that this arm movement is involved. He may quite likely be able to play the arpeggio of B major fluently in isolation; his trouble will be to fit it on the end of bar 3 and this can only be done safely if he is prepared for it in advance.   He must also remember that the whole thing must be played no faster than is consistent with absolute fluency and continuity.

Reverting to careless reading of fingering, mentioned above, there is one simple solution.   From the earliest stages the pupil must be taught to read the fingering as he reads the notes, even when reading at sight.   Correct notes and correct fingering are more or less inseparable. It is a common fault, which some teachers are inclined to overlook, for pupils to learn the notes with no attention at all to the marked fingering so that sooner or later the pernicious process of unlearning has to come into operation. Whatever else may be disregarded, notes, time, fingering and phrasing must be learned simultaneously. And the basic principles of fingering must be understood and applied from the very beginning.

Misreading of notes is in most cases due to lack of concentration or to sheer carelessness. One thing the student has to learn from the start is to use his ears, to listen to what he is doing. If a passage or a chord sounds wrong, then it is pretty certain to be wrong and the pupil must understand that when he does something which sounds wrong he must stop and work it out note by note, not let it go in the hope that the composer intended it, or that 'it'll come right next time'. It won't! Nor should he pass it over with the idea that 'teacher will put it right'. We may hope that teacher will put it right if necessary, but the pupil himself must at least try.

Teachers themselves are far from blameless at times as examiners know well enough. Augmented 2nds are frequently misread as minor 2nds –

Ex. 21

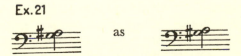

The resultant sound effect is invariably horrible, yet this particular mistake is all too common and it is obvious that the teacher is as much at fault as the pupil.

Another thoroughly pernicious and distressingly common fault is the disregard of recurring accidentals. We may perhaps forgive a young pupil for overlooking the sharpening of the F at the end of such a bar as this:

Ex. 22

But what can be done about the candidate and teacher who overlook the sharpening of the second E (quaver) in this, from a piece by Heller?

Ex. 23

Despite the unpleasant sound of the false relation between E sharp and E natural, one can rely on something like 50 per cent of candidates and their teachers not noticing it.

This kind of misreading is far from unknown in diploma examinations; there is one place in the E Major Fugue in book 2 of Bach's 'Forty-eight' where the examiner regularly clenches his teeth in readiness for a nasty aural shock. The reader may ask himself how a conscientious examiner can pass a would-be teacher who is so careless and unobservant over a perfectly elementary matter.

One final point to conclude this rather rambling chapter. Pupils must be taught to rely as much as possible on themselves. Admitted that they must also rely on the teacher – that is what he is for. But pupils must be made to realise that since the teacher in person is available only at lesson times, when they are practising they must try to be their own teacher. Too often, as suggested above, the attitude seems to be 'teacher will put it right', when with a little careful thought the pupil can put it right himself. The teacher gives the initial instruction; it is the pupil's task to endeavour to follow it. To do this he must *understand* and it is the teacher's job to ensure this understanding.

V

Lessons and Practice

Lessons have a twofold purpose, instruction and criticism. The former implies not merely the obvious teaching of specific matters such as points of technique but also the opening and broadening of the pupil's mind to music in general – his all-round musical development. The latter does not mean only the pointing out of faults or errors but, as far as may be necessary, the discussions of them, their cause and cure; and the giving of praise when due.

Lessons must be interesting, varied, even exciting, so that the pupil goes away stimulated. Too often music teachers seem to fall into two categories, (*a*) the over-earnest and (*b*) the just plain dull. Earnestness, keenness, sincerity are obvious essentials, but without humour, whether in the broader or the narrower sense of the word, they may defeat their object. Music study, though it must include a proportion of what some people would call dull technical grind, should be good fun, not a drudgery presided over by a straight-faced task-master. The dull teacher does not appreciate this and may too often be concerned with teaching more as a means of a livelihood than anything else. Admitted that we all have to make a living somehow, but if the teacher regards his work solely from this angle he has really no right to be teaching at all. Teaching should be a vocation. Its real aim should not be to collect as many fees as possible (nor to gain as many examination successes as possible) but to train and develop the minds of one's pupils to an appreciation of music and an enjoyment of the ability, even though limited, to make it.

Although it might seem more logical and practical to separate the subjects of this chapter, they are dealt with together since practice is, or should be, the outcome of what has been taught at the lessons, and lessons in any case often need to include some practice.

To what extent lessons can be planned in advance depends on circumstances; flexibility is needed but its desirability is often not realised. This is all too evident at times from what one hears in the examination room. The first thing on the programme, say the first study, may go well enough; second study not quite so well; first piece weaker and second piece verging on the poor. The reason for this is obvious enough – studies and pieces have always been taken in the same order at lessons (and at practice), so that the first study gets more attention than the second and so on, with the second piece possibly crammed in hurriedly in the last few minutes.

Normally a lesson will begin with some technical work, exercises, scales, arpeggios, partly to check on progress in the work set and partly to 'limber up'. After this the order of procedure should be varied so that each branch of the work in turn gets attention before freshness has worn off. Unless some checking-up is felt essential, it is not absolutely necessary to hear everything at every lesson; in fact, with an average pupil it is hardly possible to deal properly with exercises, scales and arpeggios, studies, pieces, sight reading and aural work in the normal half-hour lesson. If the pupil has been properly taught from the beginning, and provided that he has been set on the right lines over his study of any given piece, etc., it should be quite safe to allow him to go for a fortnight or even longer without a check. It is far better to spend a quarter of an hour on a single piece, dealing with it in detail, than to skim quickly over it in five minutes so as to make time to hear something else. At times it may be desirable to spend a whole lesson on one piece, or on one new point of study.

Not only should the order of procedure at lessons be varied, but also the point at which the pupil is told to begin a piece, study, etc. Here again the examination room often exposes weaknesses. A piece begins well enough but deteriorates gradually, this being due to the fact that the earlier part has had more practice and attention than the later. For the first week the pupil is told to practise, say, the first two lines (the examiner will probably note a date pencilled at the end of the second line); for the second week the next two lines are added (another date); and so on. At every lesson, and at every practice, the pupil starts from the beginning so that lines 1 and 2 will have had a week's more work than lines 3 and 4, a fortnight more than 5 and 6.

To begin with, chopping up a piece into two-line lengths is bad. Breaking up into complete sections, *e.g.* up to a double-bar or the end of a paragraph, is sound enough; but not stopping at the end of a bar in, probably, the middle of a phrase. Also, it means that the pupil may have to indulge in too much continuous repetition to fill out practice time. Repetition, as we know, is essential, but beyond a certain point boredom intervenes and the result is likely to be deterioration rather than improvement.

The pupil should understand that in practice he should not always begin at the beginning. In the case of youngsters the teacher may well mark points from which a start may be made. Similarly at lessons. If a two-page section has been studied, begin sometimes at a phrase halfway through the first page, or at the top of the second; in a ternary piece which has been studied all through, begin at the episode. This procedure will ensure that the whole piece, not only the earlier part, gets full attention at lessons, and its fair share of practice; it also increases the pupil's alertness. All examiners know the type of candidate who stumbles halfway through the first page but cannot pick up from that point and has to start again from the beginning. (One has bitter memories of more than one moronic diploma candidate who stumbled after nearly two pages and could not resume except from the very start.) This kind of thing may, of course, be to some extent due to the repeated instruction to 'go back to the beginning'. If a slip occurs in, say, the second or third bar, by all means go back to the beginning; but to do so because of a slip after half a page or more is ridiculous. By the time the offending passage has been reached it will have assuredly been forgotten. Some teachers insist on a return to the beginning of the phrase. This is all very well if the pupil can be trusted to know where the phrase begins, which is by no means certain in most cases. Go back to the beginning of the bar, or to the beginning of the bar before, so that there is not time for the particular snag to be lost sight of.

With the less alert pupil lessons may well include practice in beginning anywhere, just a bar or two at a time. 'Start here – stop – now start there – stop – now here.' This is hard work (why not, anyway?) but well worth it. If the pupil really knows his work, assuming reasonable intelligence, he should be able to start anywhere, even, say, on the second of a group of four semiquavers in a run, or on a chord on the fourth quaver of a bar.

Alertness may well be cultivated to some extent by insisting on the practice of scales and arpeggios starting from the top, not only from the lowest note (this applies, too, on stringed instruments), and of contrary motion scales from the extremes as well as from the middle. This, of course, is demanded in some diploma examinations but there is no need to leave it till the pupil has reached that standard. If there is a slip on the downward (or inward) run, it should not be necessary always to start again from the lowest note or from the middle of the keyboard.

It is important that any new matter, *e.g.* a technical point, should be thoroughly understood before it is left – another reason for flexibility in planning lessons. It must be explained and demonstrated and *practised by the pupil* under the teacher's eye until it is clear that he has fully grasped it and can safely be left to work at it by himself. If this takes up the whole of the lesson time, let it. Far better to let the rest of the work slide for a week than to find at the next lesson that the new matter has not been fully grasped and needs to be re-studied, with probably some unlearning to be done as well.

This sticking at one thing is a gruelling process at times but it pays dividends and not only with new matters. I recall the case of a couple of new diploma pupils whose part-playing was, to put it mildly, poor when they came to me. In both cases a whole lesson was spent dissecting a Bach fugue bar by bar with separate hands, pulling up for every single fault of part-playing, explaining, demonstrating and repeating. At the end of the lessons, both pupils and teacher were somewhat exhausted, but neither pupil has since had the slightest trouble over part-playing. They understand what it means and what it involves; accuracy in this matter can now be taken for granted.

Pulling up needs discretion. It is not always the best thing to stop the pupil every time he makes a mistake. In the cases mentioned in the preceding paragraph it was done deliberately, the pupil understanding the purpose – the solution of a purely mechanical problem. In normal circumstances continual and frequent pulling up prevents the pupil from getting any idea of the piece as a whole. Often the best plan is to hear the whole thing straight through, only stopping, if at all, for some particularly gross error. Then go through it again in detail, stopping as often as may be necessary, but not bothering about what are obviously mere accidental slips.

The teacher must be alert to spot the reason for a mistake or he will not be in a position to rectify it. The old catch phrase 'a mistake detected is half corrected' is not really true. Detection is useless unless the cause of the mistake is discovered; and then the means of correction must be found. The pupil should be encouraged to find out, as far as his limited know-ledge will allow, the cause of mistakes and even to try to suggest the remedy. Anything that he finds out for himself will 'stick' more surely than what he is just told. 'Telling shuts up the mind, questioning opens it.' In the case of misreading of notes, let him read out the names of the individual notes in the offending passage. Take the case of the misread augmented 2nd:

Ex. 24

instead of

Point to the G. 'What's that note?' 'G.' 'G what – natural, sharp, flat...?' 'Natural.' Now point to the A sharp and go through the same questions. '*Now* play them.' And alternative approach might be:

'Which note has the sharp in front of it?' 'The G.' 'Really! Is the sharp in the space or on the line?' Pupil peers closely, reading it carefully for the first time. 'Oh, on the line.' 'Right. So which note does it belong to?' 'Oh, the A of course.' 'Right – *Now* play it.' This would (or should) naturally lead to a reminder that an accidental is always on the same line or space as the note to which it refers, and also to the importance of listening – 'if it sounds wrong, it *is* wrong'.

When wrong notes are not due to misreading, the teacher must look for a physical cause. This has been dealt with on page 45 *et seq*. but it cannot be too strongly stressed that the purely physical aspect of performance, whether on the piano or anything else, is of the utmost importance. Indeed, it may be said that apart from misreading, all mechanical errors have a physical cause of some kind or other – wrong position, wrong action, wrong movement – and this is due to wrong thinking, conscious or otherwise. Refer back to Ex. 10. The wrong note at * is due to a wrong finger (*i.e.* a wrong action) and the use of this wrong finger arises from wrong thinking, not realising the change in the pattern.

Reference was made in Chapter IV to the basic physical action which involves reducing an action to its lowest and simplest terms. The same principle must often be applied in other ways. A troublesome passage must be broken down into the smallest possible sections, sections which are so short that the pupil has one thing and one thing only to think of. Refer back to Ex. 14 on page 47. The first difficulty is the 9th leap. The pupil can probably take an octave leap safely enough but has not mastered the 'feel' of a 9th. The steps are:

Ex.25

Then the closing up of the hand for the next semiquaver:

Ex.26

Think continually of the hand adjustments required and *what they feel like*.

This kind of procedure may savour of what an old friend used to call 'micro-pedagogy', but it works. The point is that the pupil starts with just one thing on which to concentrate and builds up gradually from it. The whole attention is first directed to the 9th leap and when this is mastered the attention is spread to include just one more note, and so on. Similarly with, say, a tricky shift on the violin. Practise first the shift itself, from the lower position to the higher or *vice versa*. Then add a note at either end and then integrate this into the whole phrase.

'Breaking down' must not be confined to lesson-time, it must be continued at practice so that what has been begun under the teacher's eye may be consolidated. One does not expect the pupil, at least the elementary one, to be able to work out the steps in breaking down. They must be shown at the lesson and if necessary written out in a manuscript book, on the lines of Exx. 25 and 26. A technical point mastered on these lines is as it were filed for future reference. The 'know how' is stored up and drawn on whenever appropriate. Similarly in such a case as the part-playing dealt with on page 46.

All the above should make it clear that pupils must be taught how to practise, another matter too often neglected. One sees written over a couple of bars 'practise this ten times every day', but the so-called practice may quite likely have meant playing the passage blindly with no real understanding of what is required, or the method by which it can be achieved. Even the most elementary pupils must be taught what they have to aim at and *how* to aim at it. It is useless merely to say, 'You must practise it.'

Consider the matter of finger exercises. Their object is to train and strengthen the muscles and to build up mental control. Unfortunately they are generally printed in semiquavers so that the pupil is apt to think that all that matters is speed. This is actually the last thing we want. The pupil's 'practice' consists of 'skidding through' each exercise as fast as possible, with little or no attention to hand position, correct finger action, relaxation, evenness of time and tone or any other essential. A thoughtless, mechanical process which does a lot of harm but no good at all. Practice – slow practice – at lessons, under the teacher's supervision, is essential, the pupil being made to understand *how* it is to be done, how to think, aiming always at mental control. Special difficulties must be pointed out and their solution indicated.   Only so can any real progress be expected.

The importance of slow practice and plenty of it cannot be overstressed.   In the initial stages of studying anything, it must be done sufficiently slowly to minimise the risk of error of any kind (not merely of wrong notes) – sufficiently slowly for the pupil to be able to think of everything.   Dull?   Maybe, but progress is quicker and more sure in the end.   There is always a temptation in any work which is aiming ultimately at high speed, *e.g.* scales, arpeggios, finger studies, to speed up too much too soon.   No speeding-up should be attempted until the work is completely mastered at a slow speed.   If this is done it will be found that at least reasonably high speed can be achieved with safety and comparative ease.   But the speeding-up must be gradual; it is useless to try to go from *adagio* to *presto* with no intermediate steps.

Velocity studies have a habit of providing a trap into which the majority of pupils fall with the utmost ease. They begin relatively simply, the opening bars presenting no particular problems, but get progressively more complicated.   The average pupil is deluded into starting too fast so that although the opening may go well enough, sooner or later he begins to stumble and fumble.   Steady, unvarying speed is essential and the beginning must be taken at a speed, however slow, which can be maintained throughout.   It may be well to mention again the importance of reading *everything*, including fingering and phrasing, from the very first run through, and this obviously demands slow work.

How long persistence in slow practice of any given study, piece, etc., must continue naturally depends on the pupil.   But whatever his ability – or lack of it – he can never have too much of it.

Repetition practice, especially of difficulties, must never be shirked either at practice or at lessons, dull though it may be. But it must be intelligent. Mere mechanical repetition is a waste of time. How many repetitions in any given instance depends on circumstances and on the speed with which the pupil can grasp things. 'Repeat this ten times' – or twenty times – is not necessarily a desirable instruction. A better rule is 'repeat until you can do it absolutely accurately and fluently *three or four times in succession*, it doesn't matter how slowly. And repeat the dose as soon as possible after a break.' The ability to manage a troublesome bar quite correctly once does not necessarily mean that it is mastered; but consecutive accurate renderings show that mastery is at least on the way.

A warning is needed in respect of persistence and repetition. The pupil may slip, try again, slip, try again – and slip again. The slip may be quite accidental, not due to misreading or other misunderstanding, but possibly to a touch of over-anxiety. Mere 'bashing away' is useless. Make him take his hands off the keys (or drop the bow-arm by the side) and relax completely for a few seconds, then try again. In most cases the passage will then 'go'. Pupils must be taught to do this at practice, not only when told to do so at lessons. 'Stop and go round through the gate. Don't try to force your way through the hedge – you'll only get scratched.'

The same principle must be applied to practice in general. Do not continue too long without a break (see also page 78). The earnest student may set out to do, say, three hours solid practice, but if he interprets 'solid' as meaning absolutely continuous he is liable to find himself doing more harm than good. The brain as well as the muscles needs periodical rests, so that a three-hour period should be broken at the end of, say, every half-hour, the student relaxing completely for a few minutes and so beginning again refreshed. (In the case of instrumentalists it is a good thing, too, to wash the hands, wrists and forearms well in warm water. This not only gets rid of any stickiness but also refreshes them most satisfyingly.)

It may be well to insert a note on the use of the metronome. It is sometimes used as an alleged aid to slow practice and good time-keeping, but it is of debatable value since, as experience proves, there is no guarantee that the pupil will adhere to the metronome beats. Further, it means that he is relying, or trying to rely, on some external aid instead of on his own brain. Remove the aid and he is likely to be in as bad a muddle as ever. Nor is the metronome necessarily a reliable aid to good time-keeping. This, as was shown in connection with Exx. 1 and 2, is a matter of proper understanding and application of principles. Pupils will play in incorrect time just as easily with the metronome ticking away as without it. Its sole function should be to give an indication of the desired speed of a piece, nothing else.

Practice must be planned, but as with lessons there must be flexibility. Clock-watching – five minutes for this, seven minutes for that – is not a good thing. Extra time may need to be given to new work though without entirely neglecting what is already in hand. At the same time, with young pupils it is obviously desirable that they be given some kind of (written) time-table, without being expected to adhere to it slavishly. Older pupils should be able to use their own judgement.

Pupils must be made to understand that practice involves hard work and solid concentration. Just

5

'going through' what has been set is useless. They must, as said above, be taught how to practise and must know what is to be aimed at in any given instance.

The mental attitude to difficulties is of great importance. Quite frequently one finds that a tricky passage causes a stumble not because it is in any way beyond the pupil's capabilities or because it has not been well practised, but simply through sheer funk. Students must not be allowed to overstress in their minds the difficulties they may encounter. Because a passage has given some trouble at first, the approach to it may induce some such thought as, 'Oh dear, I know I shall make a mess of it'; and naturally the mess is duly made. Alternatively, the position of the passage may not have been fixed in the mind so that it is come on unawares. The result is the same. It is essential to fix in the mind the places where special difficulties or snags occur and equally essential to be prepared for them, *but without worrying*. If the passage has been dissected and properly practised, it can be done, taken in the stride. There must be confidence. Any suggestion of 'I can't do it' or 'I'm afraid of it' must be firmly repressed. The attitude must be: 'I can and I will – and it's not as difficult as all that, anyway.'

This attitude of mind must be built up by the teacher. Take the passage to pieces at the lesson, build it up bit by bit, integrate it into its context, proving to the pupil that he can do it, however slowly. Repeat a few times with a quiet word of warning – 'Ready' – during the preceding bar. Watch for tension due to funk – 'Take it easy, take it in your stride. You can do it easily enough.' And when it is accomplished, 'Well, where's the difficulty now?'

Repetition practice, whether in such a case as the above or whether for the purpose of mastering some new point of technique, must never be hurried. Especially in the early stages ample time must be taken before each successive repetition to *think* – think what has to be done and how it is to be done.   In the dropping exercises suggested on pages 40 and 41 pupils will persist in wanting to take a new drop immediately the hand has been raised from the previous one; there is no preparation, so that the result is likely to be unsuccessful. 'Drop – raise – *stop and think* – drop...' and so on *ad lib*. In every possible way and in every possible direction the pupil must be forced to use his brains so that everything he does is intended, not merely hit or miss.   Education of any kind is not merely the assimilation of facts; it should teach the student how to think.

Students must learn to appreciate the importance of context in the correction of mistakes.   It is a distressingly frequent habit (and equally distressingly difficult to eradicate) to 'correct' a wrong note or finger by just substituting the right one and then forging ahead. Every note exists in the context which precedes and follows it and a wrong note or finger is due to an incorrect *approach*.   It may be simple enough to go on correctly when the wrong note has been put right; what matters is to approach it in such a way that no error will occur.   It is the *lead-up* to the offending spot that counts, so that the correct series of physical actions is not broken.   In a hurdle race, what matters is not so much being able to pick up and run ahead after falling over a hurdle; the thing is to be able to get over the hurdle without falling at all, *i.e.* the approach to it. Therefore – stop and *go back*, but before you start again find out what caused you to stumble; don't blunder along blindly hoping for the best.   As already mentioned, it is no good going back too far; let it be just far enough to get into the stride again.

This particular trouble, disinclination to stop and go back, needs much patience on the part of the teacher. Students at times seem congenitally incapable of doing what they are told! But here again, a solid grilling (as in the case mentioned of part-playing) may, even though rather brutal, effect a cure. In other words, once again, 'keep on telling him'.

A matter which has particular relevance to examination preparation but which is of general importance may be dealt with here – the length of time to be spent working at any given piece or study. It is not, of course, possible to make any suggestions in terms of weeks or months, but the teacher must exercise great discretion in order that too prolonged study may not lead to boredom or worse. After more than forty years I still remember the case of a small girl of about eleven who came to me for piano lessons when I was quite a young teacher. She played a piece, very badly, and I asked how long she had been working at it. 'Eighteen months'. 'Do you like it?' 'I HATE IT!' Comment is hardly needed.

Short, elementary pieces cannot stand up to prolonged study; indeed, if the pupil has been well trained at the beginning they should not need it. It is not essential to get everything right up to concert or examination standard, though there is no need to go to the other extreme and be content with a merely sketchy knowledge. Watch continually for signs of boredom and if they become apparent drop the piece at least for the time being. Bear in mind that examinations or no examinations the youngster should build up something of a repertoire and cover as much varied ground as to style, etc., as is possible. It is rather shaming for the child who is asked to play to friends of the family yet has to admit that he has forgotten the pieces he played at his last examination and has not yet mastered those for the next – and does not know any others. Aim always at ample variety even though perfection in performance may not be achieved.

Teaching examination papers sometimes include a question on the treatment of adult pupils as compared with children, implying, of course, that the adult is at an elementary stage. Fundamentally there is little if any difference. The adult is musically a child and must be treated as such. Certainly one does not need to employ such simple terminology as with the child, though there is no harm in doing so, and it may help to go into greater detail over the 'reason why'. Adults and children who are at the same approximate level of musical development all have to learn the same fundamentals in the same way, and the adult may not necessarily display any quicker perception than the child; in some cases, considerably less!

It is rather easy unconsciously to assume that the adult, because of mature years, has a wider musical background than the child, but this is not always so. Even if he has a fair background, he still has to learn the correct hand position, correct holding of violin and bow, how to relax the throat muscles and so on. Take nothing for granted and do not be afraid of simple, elementary terminology. To tell an adult to 'relax the wrist' after dropping into a chord may be no more effective than with a small child. Tell him to 'let it flop' and it will.

A final point with regard to advanced work which may well be borne in mind by any advanced students who may read this book. The really big works cannot be learned in a hurry. This is really self-evident, yet is comparatively rarely realised by either teachers or students. A student who is technically adequate may master the notes of such a work as the 'Appassionata' Sonata or the Beethoven Violin Concerto in a matter of weeks; it is a mere matter of mechanical ability and dexterity. What he will not have even begun to master, unless he is phenomenally gifted, is the meaning of the work. He will not have 'got inside it'. One gets wearied of people who come along saying, 'I must do my F.T.C.L. (or L.R.A.M. or other advanced diploma) in three months' time', when they have only been working at their programme for a fortnight or so – if that. They may be able to learn the notes accurately and fluently enough (or they may not) but they will not *know* the works. Not months but years of study are needed for such works as the two mentioned above, and equally for others of far less technical difficulty but of equal musical and emotional content. A student may be able to sight read accurately such a piece as the Eighth Prelude of Bach's 'Forty-eight', but he will not probe its depths in a mere month or two. (Piano teachers may well ponder the subtleties of Mozart's well-known Rondo in A minor – so deceptively simple on the surface yet to the sincere musician a cause of many outsize headaches.) With all really great works the more one works at them and thinks about them, the more one finds in them. The late sonatas of Beethoven, the Chromatic Fantasia and Fugue of Bach, the D minor Violin Sonata of Brahms, for example, seem almost bottomless. One can study and probe and study and probe and still find something new, something of which one had not before realised the full significance.

Such works then, whether for examination purposes or not, must be studied, put aside, re-studied and put aside again. During the rest periods the subconscious mind will be working over them and when they are taken up again there will be deeper insight (one postulates, naturally, a really musical student) and, of course, greater technical facility. Only thus can they become adequately presentable for public performance.

VI

Technique

THERE is a tendency in some quarters to decry the study of technique as such. 'If you study too much technique you will kill your musicianship.' Such people may be recommended to study the lives or memoirs of great executants, noting what they did, whether in their student days or later, in the way of technical study and practice, and asking themselves to what extent it 'killed' their musicianship. Rachman-inoff, for example, recounts the way he was trained in his early days – technique and ever more technique; yet he became one of the greatest pianists of his generation. Von Bülow, no mean performer, said: 'The first thing a pianist needs is technique; the second thing a pianist needs is technique; and the third thing a pianist needs is technique.' For pianist substitute violinist, singer, organist, what you will, the same thing applies.

Although one may get the impression that some great executants were, as it were, born with a ready-made technique, they have nevertheless had to cultivate it. Liszt has been described as a pianist 'by the grace of God' – but he still had to practise. I may recall a story of him told me by my own teacher. The master, as an old man, was staying with friends near London preparing for a recital. One morning he shut himself in the music room and the children of the house clustered round outside the door expecting to hear all kinds of fireworks and virtuosity. At lunch their father asked, 'Well, and did you hear the great Abbé Liszt practising?' 'Yes – but he played everything *so slowly*!'

Technique, as has already been remarked, is mainly mental. In fact (as may be deduced by the intelligent reader from all that has so far been written) everything in study or performance is 'mainly mental', whether it is a matter of mere 'learning' or of control. In everything the teacher must be continually hammering home 'Use your brains; think.' Many people are inclined to look upon technique as implying mere mechanical ability and, in particular, agility. This is far too narrow an outlook. We say that So-and-so has a colossal technique simply because he can fire off double octaves like a machine-gun, or can cover double stoppings as fast as any reasonable violinist can cover single notes. But technique means far more than this kind of thing. It means everything except the actual musical interpretation, in other words, everything on the physical/mechanical side of performance, including not merely agility but control of dynamics, control of tone-colour and other less obvious matters. (We note again *control* – 'mainly mental'.) Interpretation involves the application of variation of dynamics, variations of colour (and a hundred other things) but the performer cannot achieve the application of them unless he has the technique to do so.

There is, incidentally, the technique of composition – the ability to write music in such a way that it expresses the composer's thought in the most effective and practical (or practicable) manner. One hears at times compositions of which a legitimate criticism is that although the basic thought and intention are good, yet they are not effectively expressed; they do not 'come off' properly. The composer's technique is inadequate. His knowledge of harmony and counterpoint (not merely in the academic sense) may be insufficient, or his understanding of an appropriate and idiomatic style of writing for a particular instrument.

Technical study must begin from the very first lesson. In the case of the piano, correct position and muscular condition of fingers, hands and arms.   In the case of a stringed instrument, correct posture and holding of the instrument.   On the piano, proper use of the fingers in simple exercises for a true *legato*; on the violin, drawing the bow at right angles to the strings.

It is not for a moment suggested that any but a few pupils can achieve a 'big technique', but even those who can never hope to rise above, say, the level of grade V or VI should have a *good* technique within the inevitable limits.   There is no reason why they should not, provided that their basic training has been on the right lines from the start.

There are those who are inclined to say: 'All this dull technical study – what's the good of it?   I shall never be a Rachmaninoff or a Menuhin.'   Quite.   But unless you have a technique adequate, or rather, more than adequate, to cope with what you want to play, how can you hope to play it decently?

All examiners know the kind of elementary candidate who cannot manage even a fair rendering of simple finger exercises, or scales, or studies, because their hand position and finger action have never been given proper attention.   Equally they know the diploma candidate whose idea of practice has obviously just blind, un-thinking repetition with no intelligence, no control, no muscular development.   In fact, one might almost make a comparison with someone who tries to solve a quadratic equation when he does not understand simple multiplication and division.   Or the person who prefers to try to push his way through the hedge rather than go round through a convenient gate. Whatever we want to do, however elementary it may be, we *must* have adequate technique.

One is sometimes irritated by some such remark as, 'Of course, she hasn't much technique but she plays so musically.' She cannot play musically unless her technique is adequate for what she is playing. One notices, too, that in such cases the person concerned is apt to tackle works which are beyond her technical ability so that musicality is anyway lost in the struggle to cope with the bare notes.

The aim of technical study, whether elementary or advanced, should be to get the playing apparatus into such a condition of efficiency that it functions unconsciously, the conscious mind being thus freed to concentrate on interpretation. A stock of technical ability is gradually built up and stored away, to be drawn on as and when needed. The idea of 'getting your technique only from your pieces' is of very debatable value. There are times, of course, when a passage in a particular piece has to be broken down so that its particular difficulties are mastered. (See Ex. 14 and the method of practising it at Exx. 25 and 26.) But the basic technique itself can only be acquired and mastered by working at it first in isolation, starting from a basic exercise.

Technique needs to be treated to a large extent as a separate study, especially in the initial stages of any aspect of it. (This, I know, may be considered rank heresy by some, but my own personal experience as both student and teacher proves the accuracy of the statement.) 'Play-ways', so beloved of some 'up-to-date' teachers, may be all very well, but the old method of hard work and concentration on basic essentials produces better and quicker results. Take, as a simple example, the matter of achieving a true *legato* in finger-work. You may, if you like, give the little pupil small pieces in the five-finger position, all next-door notes, and explain to him that each finger must rise as the next one goes down – which, of course, it must. But he has too much to think about – notes, note-values, counting and so on. The basic physical action must first be studied in isolation. Use the analogy of the see-saw – you sit on one end and the other comes up. Then see-saw with two fingers on two next-door notes, starting with the most easily controlled fingers, second and third, concentrating on the up movement of each finger in turn, and what it feels like. Do this with each pair of fingers in turn. Then proceed to three-finger groups:

Ex.27

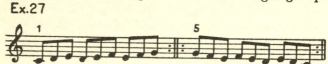

always concentrating on the up movement. It helps if the teacher keeps saying 'Up, up, up'. Next go on to the complete five-finger group, both straight up and down and in varied order:

Ex.28

By this time the idea should have taken root, it will have 'clicked', and the pupil is ready for his little *legato* pieces. This method is, obviously, very much 'one thing at a time'. It may be argued that it is old-fashioned and dull. Maybe. But achieves far quicker and safer results than any play-way ever invented.

Some educationists seem to suggest that simple

arithmetic may be learned by 'playing at shops'. But how can the child work out the cost of two packets of chocolate at 7d. a packet unless he has already mastered his 'two-times table'? Such a basic exercise as that suggested in the preceding paragraph corresponds to this table. The essential thing is to begin always from something utterly simple which the pupil cannot fail to grasp and which will act as a foundation. (Refer back to the use of a simple 'drop', page 40.)

At a more advanced level, take hand (wrist) *staccato*. In essence this involves a vibration of the hand from the wrist-joint, the movement being as small as is consistent with effectiveness and clarity. The first step is to fix in the mind the 'feel' of this movement, to which end some exaggeration may help. Hold the forearm loosely horizontal, the hand hanging loosely from the wrist. Raise and lower the hand several times slowly with the wrist as a pivot, forearm unmoving. This is the basic action. Now quicken the movement at the same time making it smaller. Think of shaking a pepper-pot. This introduces what the pupil can understand as vibration. Now to the keyboard in a series of *rhythmical* exercises:

Ex. 29

Each of these should be done with each finger in turn, hands separately, beginning with the easiest finger, the third. Keep close to the keys, loose and avoid any movement of finger from knuckle ('don't flap your fingers!').   It is a hand action, not a finger one.   When this is mastered go on to short five-finger exercises and one- and two-octave scales.

A very important point arises from consideration of the above – the cultivation of sticking power. This particular branch of technique is apt to induce quick tiring; the arm begins to ache and to stiffen, and eventually the whole apparatus 'locks'. Hence the necessity of *graduated* exercises such as those suggested. (If you want to become a good cross-country runner you will hardly begin your training with a twenty-mile trot.)   The resistance to tiring must be built up step by step and this involves, among other things, a deliberate fight against the natural tendency for the arm and wrist muscles to stiffen.   (Remember, too, that tension may arise from over-anxiety to avoid it.)   When Ex. 29 is under control, it is no use going straight on to four-octave scales; one octave is quite enough for a start.

The principle of gradual building up obviously operates at all levels, and as well as physical sticking-power, the mental has also to be considered, more especially with young students.   (Remember what was said on page 64 about periodical breaks in a practice period.)   The child cannot concentrate for more than a limited length of time and his ability to do so has to be nursed along. This is one reason why elementary studies and pieces are always short.   It is not good policy to say 'Practise this finger exercise twenty times running'; after half a dozen repetitions concentration will almost certainly begin to weaken and the attention to wander.   Better to say, 'Do it four times, then rest, then another four, then rest again.'   And so on. Short bursts of properly concentrated effort.   Older students, too, need warning over this.   The really keen student may just 'slog away' time after time without intermission, not realising that without periodical and frequent rests his work will begin to deteriorate rather than to improve.

The principle of gradual building-up again is seen in the accepted progression from, say, the finger exercises to the scale and the scale to the study. Early finger exercises are short and simple and adhere normally to the repetition of one pattern. Scales require more sticking power and introduce complications of fingering, but each scale still repeats, two or three or four times, the pattern of its first octave. The study goes farther, requiring still more sticking power and introducing all kinds of variation of pattern and consequent complications of fingering. The problems, such as they are, are cumulative and the process shows an application of what was said on cumulativeness in Chapter III. Note also what was said on page 63 about the common trap in many velocity studies.

It is perhaps worth pointing out that the same principles apply in paper work. One method of teaching elementary-chord progression is to begin with practice in writing cadences, just two chords in each case. Exercises which follow will be very short, five or six chords only. As more resources are mastered, the exercises will lengthen and the complications increase – cumulation again. But we have to begin with something absolutely basic, in this case the cadence, on which we build the technique of handling chords.

Reference has more than once been made to relaxation in piano playing. It applies equally on any other instrument and in singing. The word is not infrequently misinterpreted as meaning flabbiness. Possibly the only time we are completely relaxed is when we lie flat on our backs in bed. As soon as we use a muscle it tenses to a greater or less extent and the essential point in musical performance is that this tension must be the minimum required to produce the effect at which we are aiming. Whatever we do, except when lying in bed, we can never have all our muscles completely relaxed.

If we let the hand and arm hang loosely by the side, the muscles from the shoulder downwards are relaxed. As soon as we bring the hand into the playing position on the keyboard, muscles operate. Shoulder muscles function to keep the upper arm in position; upper arm muscles control the forearm; forearm muscles prevent the wrist from sagging and so on. But all these muscles must be exerted only to the minimum extent needed to keep hand and arm in the correct position. Over-exertion, undue tension, leads to quick tiring and loss of facility and agility. Similarly with holding the violin. To keep the elbow under the instrument involves exertion of shoulder muscles and causes some tension in the upper arm, but this tension must be reduced to the absolute minimum. Tension in the upper arm reacts right down into the fingers, with deleterious results. This is easily realised if we hold the forearm out horizontally and deliberately stiffen the upper arm; immediate loss of control of the fingers will be felt.

It is, of course, useless to talk to young pupils about relaxation; the word must be looseness. With ample demonstration and guided practice it can quite easily be achieved. But it must be dealt with from the very beginning so that bad habits are not allowed to form. More than one writer has remarked that the small child's hand and arm are 'naturally' relaxed. Experience does not always bear out this statement. Some children find all too little difficulty in stiffening.

Comparison of the right way with the wrong way is

often helpful.   Drop hand and arm by the side, quite flabby.   Deliberately stiffen the muscles and realise the different sensation.

Exaggerated and needless movements are to be avoided except for special purposes.   Letting the wrist 'flop' after each note or chord in the early stages of 'dropping' exercises is quite sound, but it must be understood that it is only a safeguard against key-bedding (or after-pressure).   Once the sound has arrived, any further downward impulse into the keys is so much wasted energy and the complete relaxation of the wrist enables the pupil to appreciate this.   Once the knack of resting on the key-beds rather than continuing to press down on them is mastered, the 'flop' should be dispensed with – it becomes a needless movement.   This looks rather like unlearning, but the method always works.

Staccato is a very frequent source of exaggerated, sometimes ridiculously exaggerated movements. There are still teachers who appear to believe in what one writer used to call 'full wrist *staccato*'.   After each note the hand is pulled back more or less vertically from the wrist.   What results, except bad ones, this is intended to produce one cannot say.   The 'pull back' stiffens the fingers, wrist and forearm and in any case the hand has only to go all the way back again for the next note, with a probable mis-hit.   No speed, of course, is possible.   The same extraordinary procedure is often found at ends of phrases and for rests in such cases as this:

Ex.30

etc.

(which unfortunately is marked in at least one little examination book 'Down, up, down, up'). Keep close to the keys; just let each key bring the finger up with it. DON'T FLAP!

Every teacher knows the kind of pupil who is suffering from bad instruction from a former teacher and whose technical ideas, if any, are comprehensively on the wrong lines. As has already been said, patching up is useless. Go right back to the beginning and rebuild on a proper foundation. Explain, discreetly, why this is necessary – but try to avoid obvious and overt criticism of the previous teacher.

It is not suggested that this chapter covers completely the teaching of technique or of any one branch of it. The aim has been to show general, basic principles and method, with a sufficient number of practical examples to illustrate them. Let it be stressed again that correct principles and methods must be built up from the very first lesson. 'Begin as you mean to go on.'

VII

Aural Work

WHETHER there is any intrinsic value in the kind of aural work which the average pupil does merely with an examination in view is perhaps debatable. This is not to be understood as a denigration of aural training as such – far from it – but one is inclined to wonder what value there is in distinguishing, say, between a major and a minor 3rd as intervals isolated from a musical context.

With whatever aim aural training is undertaken, realisation of the principles enunciated in chapter III is essential, particularly those of memory and cumulativeness. The perennial problem is how to set about the training in the limited portion of a weekly half-hour lesson which can be made available, plus the fact that the pupil cannot always do any kind of 'practice' himself. As will be shown, there are some things which he can actually practise, but in the case of, say, rhythm tests, tapping out the note-values of a passage played to him, he cannot, unless he is lucky enough to have somebody at home who will co-operate.

The first thing to be realised is that aural training, like everything else, is fundamentally based on memory, so that repetition and frequent renewal of impressions are essential. Say the pupil is learning to identify the notes of a major triad (which he cannot do, incidentally, unless he can first appreciate whether one note is higher or lower than another). The triad will be played many times at various pitches, both in slow arpeggio and as a chord, so that he can begin to realise what it sounds like. Next he may sing each note in the usual order, as the teacher plays it – C, E, G, C, – and then be made to sing alone the arpeggio using letter names, figures (1, 3, 5, 8) or tonic solfa (see below) as the teacher prefers, after the tonic has been sounded. He may also sing the tonic followed by each note in turn – C, E; C, G; C, C. Note the 'one thing at a time', step-by-step procedure. All this, slow as it may seem, will gradually impress the sound effects on his memory and from the last step he may proceed to identifying the sounds as in the actual test. A deeper impression may be made by reversing the test, *i.e.* playing a tonic and asking him to sing or hum one of the notes of the chord.

A similar procedure must be followed whatever the type of test being dealt with, always starting with the simplest and most basic thing. Rhythm-tapping, for example, must be preceded by exercises in tapping out regular pulsation in twos, threes and fours; then the subdivision of just one beat may be introduced, – *e.g.*

; then subdivision of two beats –

. (At least one book, quoting von

Bülow's dictum that 'in the beginning was rhythm', states that all children have inborn sense of rhythm. Experience proves that despite von Bülow this is highly debatable.)

The cumulative aspect must not be overlooked. I have already referred to the question of a foolproof method of recognising modulations by ear. To reach this fairly advanced stage of aural work, all the earlier, elementary steps, even as far back as recognising the notes of a major or a minor triad, must have been mastered. There is no short cut to this or to anything else.

With regard to practice outside the lesson, a good deal is possible even without help from somebody at home. In the case, say, of the major triad (see above), examples of this triad may be written out in semibreves on manuscript paper. The pupil is told to imitate what has been done at the lesson, *i.e.* play the triads, slowly, listening carefully. Then to play them again, singing each note as he plays it, and so on. He may also say, 'I'll sing the third note.' He plays the tonic (from the music), attempts to sing the third note and checks accuracy by then playing it. Similarly with the recognition of intervals at a later stage. Write out, for example, a large number of major and minor 3rds, marking clearly which is which. At practice the pupil plays slowly and, listening carefully, a series of major 3rds, followed by a series of minor ones. Then he may play major followed by minor on the same note, realising clearly which he is playing in every case. The distinction will gradually become clear to him. Again the procedure may be reversed – play a note and sing a major or minor 3rd above it, checking at the keyboard.

In the end, whatever method is adopted and whatever book may be used as a guide, it all boils down to hammering sound effects into the memory by repetition.

Tonic solfa, though considered out of date by some, is undoubtedly an enormous help since it builds up a strong feeling for relative pitch. (As a small child I had it hammered into me at school *via* the Modulator, and despite my absolute pitch I can still find it useful.) If used, however, it must be taught thoroughly and accurately. This is an obvious statement but it is made since in examining one not infrequently finds that although a young candidate may know the terminology – doh, ray, me, etc. – he does not necessarily understand its application. If properly understood it solves innumerable difficulties.

Care is needed over talk about 'mental effects'. The 'scrunchy' effect of a major 7th or the 'squashy' one of a minor 2nd (or however one cares to describe them) are safe enough. But such statements as 'the major triad is bright, the minor triad is sad' or that the major key is happy and the minor sad, are risky. I recall two eminent examiners talking at lunch and one of them made the latter statement (he should have known better!). The reply flashed back 'What about the "Dead March in Saul?"' Chopin's C minor Nocturne, at least in the minor key sections, is certainly sad enough; but what of the scherzo-like Second Fugue of Bach's 'Forty-eight'?

One point that does need stressing, and not only in connection with aural work, is the importance of listening to the bass. It arises most obviously in connection with such matters as identifying cadences (though here again playing examples of any given cadence in various keys and with varied arrangements of the upper parts, to impress the effect on the memory, is essential) and singing the lower part of a two-part passage. In both cases the pupil must at first be helped by emphasising the bass so that his attention is forced to it. The preparation for two-part passages begins with single intervals, consonant at first, the lower note being well emphasised. Then two consecutive intervals, then three, with the lower part emphasis gradually diminished. The pupil must be urged to try not to hear the upper part at all (impossible, of course, but it will set him thinking on the right lines) – to direct the whole of his attention to the lower one. Much trouble may arise because the pupil overstresses the difficulty; he thinks he cannot do it. The suggestions just made should help to counteract this.

Listening to the bass or, indeed, listening to anything but the melody, does need intensive cultivation. As another personal reminiscence, I recall a class many years ago. We were all professional students and most of us were pretty well advanced in our practical work, while at least a few of us were not a little proud of possessing absolute pitch. The lecturer played on the piano a slow tune in the bass with quick movement above it in the right hand. When asked to identify the left-hand tune, not one of us had spotted that it was the 'National Anthem'. It was a remarkably cogent lesson in listening. The top part, like the right hand, always pulls the attention to itself. (How many listeners to Wagner's *Meistersinger* Overture ever really hear the *Mastersinger* theme when it appears in the bass at the well-known passage where three themes are combined?)

It is well not to be misled by the pupil who has absolute pitch, or to feel that on that account there is no need to bother about aural training. Even though he may be able to identify any note by its sound, he must still know exactly what constitutes a major 3rd or a minor triad. And absolute pitch is of no help in rhythm tests, nor does it necessarily ensure the ability to sing the lower of two parts. One has often found diploma candidates who sail happily through all the tests based on relative pitch but who lose marks in the rhythm test.

The development of mental hearing, *i.e.* the ability to hear in the imagination the sound of what is read on paper, is often a problem even though in theory it should not be. Although the reader of this book can grasp the significance of what he is reading at the present moment, he does not (one hopes) need to read it aloud nor, indeed, to imagine the sound of each word. The meaning is understood from the mere sight of the words. But he can, if he chooses, imagine the sounds of the words, hearing them silently. This is what is meant by mental hearing and it is what we need to be able to do with music. Words can convey meaning quite apart from their spoken sound, whether actual or imagined. Music exists only in sound.

Development of mental hearing, of the 'inner ear', must arise from the normal processes of aural training and involves, of course, the memory, with an unlimited amount of repetition practice. The reason why we have no difficulty in mentally hearing the words we read is that we are dealing with them continually from the time we first begin our education. We learn, for example, how to spell 'me,' what it signifies and how to pronounce it, and we repeat it so often that we have no trouble in imagining its sound when we see it written or printed. The same process is needed in music. As a simple example, the pupil learns to recognise, say, the major 3rd by playing it, singing it or hearing it played a large number of times. He must also be able to recognise it on paper. If he can do this he can sing it, and if he can sing it aloud then he should be able to 'sing it silently'. This is admittedly a very simple and elementary example but it demonstrates the principles and the procedure. It must, of course, be stressed that accurate mental hearing is impossible unless what is seen on the printed page is understood and can be recognised for what it is through the eye. One cannot 'imagine' a major 3rd or a perfect cadence from the notation unless one can recognise them as such.

Since this is a book on general principles it is not proposed to deal in further detail with aural work. The suggestions in this chapter should at least help the teacher to handle it in a way which will, if followed with care and thoughtfulness, produce adequate results. It has to be admitted that some pupils, while not exactly tone-deaf, seem to offer but little possibility of aural development. Nevertheless, at least something can and should be done.

VIII

Sight Reading

FACILITY in instrumental sight reading depends mainly on quickness of physical reaction to visual *stimuli*. The music 'goes in through the eye and comes out at the fingers'. Good sight reading postulates high-speed and accurate reactions, and here we are really at the mercy of the individual pupil. The 'stodgy' pupil, whose reactions are in any case relatively slow, may perhaps be an accurate and careful reader but is unlikely ever to achieve any great fluency simply because of his natural handicap, though improvement is possible through practice.

The natural sight reader also may present a problem. Owing to his inborn facility and quick reactions he may tend to be slack over detail and to trust to his instinctive ability to 'get by'. He may be slipshod or even lazy over his practice, needing a very tight rein.

(The same may occur with the type of pupil who is blessed (or cursed) with what a colleague of mine used to call 'natural flashy fluency'. He can cover the notes with considerable facility and with but little trouble, but may be distinctly careless over accuracy and neatness of detail.)

It is hardly necessary to mention the usual bits of advice – look at the clefs, key-signature, time-signature and so on. What must be stressed is the importance of fluency and continuity, whatever the speed. Stumbling and fumbling, stopping to correct mistakes, must be avoided, at least in the examination room.   Keep going at all costs.

In my own view much weakness in sight reading is due to the fact that the player just does not 'know his notes' sufficiently well.   Instead of the sight of the symbol on paper producing immediately the correct corresponding reaction on the keyboard or the finger-board, he has to think too consciously what the notes are and what are their time-values, and this even allowing for varying speeds of mental/physical reactions. When the beginner 'learns his notes' he must be kept at it until real fluency and assurance are achieved.   It is all too easy to try to push on the beginner too far too soon.   Exercises in note-finding and note-identifi-cation, dull though they may be, must be persisted in until reactions are instantaneous.   The teacher should be able to say 'Play F – play middle C' and so on, and the pupil should do so without a trace of hesitation.   The fingers should adjust themselves automatically on key-board or fingerboard, without need of conscious thought.   Similarly the teacher should be able to point to any note on the stave – 'Play that – now that...' – with instantaneous response.   Only so can the pupil who is not a born sight reader (and of course there are such) be assured of at least reasonable progress.   As long as there has to be conscious effort to think things out, no proper fluency can be expected.

(It may possibly be objected that there is no such thing as a 'born sight reader' and if we insist on exact literalism, there is not.   But the term serves its purpose well enough.   Such a person is one whose memory is quick and retentive and whose mental/physical re-actions are exceptionally quick.)

In the case of singers it is obvious that sight-reading ability depends mainly if not entirely on aural development and for this Tonic solfa is of the greatest help. Singing teachers are apt to complain that a pupil's sight reading is poor not realising that they themselves may be at fault through neglecting aural work.   Here again there is no royal road, no short cut.   The matter has to be dealt with step by step from the lowest level.

In the elementary stages the piano student normally works first at passages consisting entirely of next-door notes, so that he has simply to watch direction, up or down.   Then occasional 3rds are introduced, then 4ths, and so on.   This 'reading by interval' is most helpful. Exactly the same procedure can be followed with singers, but they must first be able to sing a major scale, ascending or descending.

Sight reading must never be neglected either at lessons or at practice, but care is needed over choice of material.   Too often the tendency is to use material which is technically far too difficult for its purpose. It is not uncommon to find, say, a grade VI pupil, using pieces of the same grade for sight practice.   The material used must be easy enough for the pupil to have at least some chance of achieving fluency and accuracy, well below the standard of difficulty of the kind of thing he is studying for repertoire.   In some cases really drastic measures are needed and it may be found desirable to give to a pupil whose performance is of diploma standard something like grade II pieces for sight reading.   This may deflate his *ego* but it will help his reading enormously.   The pupil must first have something with which he can cope quite easily so that he will acquire the habit of fluency and at the same time his self-confidence will be built up.

Self-confidence – I can and I will – is as important in sight reading as in anything else.   The student who says 'I know I'm a bad reader' will never be anything else. (Compare what was said on page 66 regarding the approach to difficulties.)

Any kind of ensemble work, duet-playing, accompanying, etc., is all to the good for the improvement of sight reading, as are also a knowledge of harmony and musical structure. The main thing is to keep at it regularly, frequently and conscientiously.

IX

Examinations

DESPITE occasional sneers from highbrow musicians (who should know better) about 'peripatetic examiners' and pot-hunting (certificate-hunting would be more strictly accurate), there is nothing intrinsically wrong with the kind of examination system administered by such institutions as Trinity College, London, the Royal Schools of Music or the Australian Music Examinations Board. What is wrong is the misuse, one may even say abuse, of the system BY teachers, often egged on and abetted by parents.

It is an unfortunate fact, which may be stated quite bluntly, that some teachers appear to look on the aim of music teaching simply as a matter of preparing pupils for one examination after another – and nothing else. They talk volubly about the number of candidates they have entered, the number of honours or merit certificates their pupils have received. But the idea of music study as a means of broadening the mind or as a source of enjoyment is never, apparently, considered. To their pupils music study can never be fun; it tends to be looked upon as a possibly unwelcome extension of school work, directed solely to taking one examination after another and to the acquisition of more and more certificates to be exhibited to admiring relations and friends.

Parents unfortunately may show a similar deplorable attitude (recall the earlier reference to the status symbol). The child learns because mother says he must and mother (or father, or both) insists on an examination every year. If the result is not up to parental expectations, the teacher, whatever his own attitude to the matter, is likely to get a more-in-sorrow-than-in-anger phone call implying that it is his fault that the result is not better. This may, of course, be so; but many .parents seem quite incapable of realising, or are at least unwilling to realise, that the child may have been handicapped for practice-time, may have been bothered by school examinations, or may through pressure of other matters have been simply too tired.

Digressing for a moment, one cannot forbear to mention the way in which some parents overload their children. On top of regular school work, involving homework, after-school games, etc., there may be music study, speech, dancing in the case of girls, choir work and possibly other things as well. So that it is literally impossible for the child to cope adequately with any one thing, much less with the lot. What the poor teacher can do in such cases is a problem. The obviously honest thing would be to risk giving offence and say, 'I will not take this pupil; he has too much on his plate already.' But this will only mean that the child will be sent to some other teacher who has fewer scruples. All one can do is to make things as easy as possible for the victim, to be content with only moderate progress and to dig one's heels in over examinations.

It is important for the teacher (and the parents, if they can be brought to see the light) to understand the true function and aim of examinations – to look on them as a means, not as an end. There is much criticism at times of examinations of all kinds, not only in music, but nobody has yet been able to suggest anything which will replace them satisfactorily. The grade examination performs several useful functions. It acts as an incentive, giving the pupil a definite aim, something to work for. Many children, more especially those who are not naturally interested in music, need such an incentive. Without it they will never do their best but will tend to take things too easily.

The examination offers an independent and objective assessment of the quality of the work of both pupil and teacher and helps to keep them 'on their toes'. The examiner's reports can point out weaknesses not only in the pupil but in the teacher's method, weaknesses which might otherwise not be realised. Further, examination syllabuses offer a ready-made scheme for a graded course of study which can obviously be of great help to the young and inexperienced teacher.

The attitude of teachers and candidates to the examiner is of much importance. The examiner is a critic but, let it be noted, a benevolent one. Too many teachers and candidates seem to regard him as a natural enemy. Success means that you have defeated him; failure that he has defeated you. This is a hopelessly wrong attitude. To be quite frank, it does not matter in the slightest to the examiner whether the candidate performs well or badly, whether he passes or fails – except that bad candidates are a strain on his nerves and temper. He naturally takes his work seriously, but is entirely objective and nothing personal enters into the matter. His job is simply to assess the quality of the work presented, to allot the marks and offer the comments which he deems appropriate and, circumstances permitting, to suggest methods of improvement where necessary. He does not like giving low marks or having to write caustically critical comments. It is no pleasure at all to have to listen to bad work. Only those who have experienced it can appreciate the exhaustion felt at the end of a period of it. Nerves are on edge and one probably has incipient writer's cramp. (This is not, by the way, intended to be a hard-luck story; it does not happen all the time!)

The type of examiner who still existed in my own student days, whose aim seemed to be to find out what the candidate did not know and fail him on that, rather than to give him credit for what he did know, has died out. I can recall examiners who were notorious for their manner, more or less terrifying all the candidates and reducing the girls to tears. As a student I sat for a very advanced performer's diploma. There were three examiners, all with well-known names and all known for their unhelpful attitude to candidates. The whole time I was playing (from memory, of course) the senior member of the trio was pacing up and down the room, continually crossing my line of sight, with his hands behind his back and a grim frown on his face. When I was about three-quarters of the way through the biggest piece in my programme – I believe it was the 'Waldstein' Sonata – a gruff voice suddenly ejaculated, 'All right, that's enough o' that', so that my immediate reaction was 'Failed!' This kind of thing would never happen now. Nobody was more surprised than I to find that I had passed.

Another notorious character was a well-known adjudicator of singing at competitions. If a competitor stood up and produced bad work, he had been known to get up and yell, 'Why do you come here wasting my time? GET OUT!!!' One may imagine the perturbetion of the secretary (and everybody else) if that were to happen now.

In parenthesis I may perhaps recount a favourite

story of the late Sir Granville Bantock. He was examining in the north of England. In came a sturdy little Yorkshire lad for a low grade, removed his jacket, rolled up his sleeves and attacked the piano with vigour and confidence. All the time he was playing he continually twisted his face about, with his jaws working round and round. After the examination was finished, Sir Granville said, 'Tell me, sonny, why do you keep on making faces [imitating him] all the time you're playing?' Back came the reply, 'Goom – gives me ploock!' This at least showed some idea of the right approach.

The wrong attitude to the examiner is well illustrated by my own experience at the first convent I visited on an examination tour of India. I may say that I had never been to India before and all that teachers there knew of me was what they may have deduced from reading some of my earlier books. Personally I was quite unknown to them. After greeting me, the teacher said, 'Oh Dr. Lovelock, we hear you're a very *strict* examiner.' To which I replied: 'What do you mean by "strict?" Do you expect me to rap the children over the knuckles every time they play a wrong note? Or do you think I'm going to try to frighten them?' What she probably meant was that I demand a high standard, which admittedly I do. But at the back of the teacher's remark was a certain fear of the unknown which was quite needless. I may add that this teacher (a nun) and I soon became firm friends and I used to look forward to my annual visit to her convent. And I think that she and her pupils used to look forward to having me there.

Naturally, when an examiner goes to a centre for the first time everybody is wondering 'What's he like?' If the teacher knows his job and the candidates are well trained, what is there to worry about? Even if the work is not as good as it should be, the examiner is not going to be personally offended, though his opinion (objective, let it again be stressed) will be reflected in the marks he awards. Examiners are not ogres though some people seem to think they are! As I have sometimes explained to nervous candidates, they neither bark nor bite.

Another teacher, in Malaya this time, annoyed me greatly (and here I was justified in feeling annoyed) by saying, 'I told her if she did that the examiner would be cross.' Of course the poor child had naturally 'done that' in the examination through sheer dread of me being 'cross'. This kind of thing makes any examiner furious, though his feelings will not be reflected in his personal attitude to the candidates.

I have dealt at some length with the approach to the examination and the examiner since the attitudes exposed are none too rare and the examiner can do little to eradicate them unless he is able to address a teachers' meeting.

Another point to be mentioned is the not uncommon tendency to put the blame for a poor result on the wrong shoulders, including, perhaps, those of the examiner himself. His standard is too high, he was in a bad temper (he wasn't and even if he were he would not let his marking reflect it), the children were frightened of him. If they were frightened of him, whose fault was it? Certainly not his, but almost certainly that of the teacher or the parents. To put it colloquially, some teachers and parents will fuss so. The candidate arrives in ample time with teacher or parent and during the wait in the ante-room there is a continual barrage of, 'You're all right, dear, aren't you? You're not NERVOUS?' Frocks are patted down, ties straightened, hair combed and so on until the poor child develops sheer funk through no fault of his or her own. Unless the child is too young to look after himself it is generally far better to let him come to the examination un-accompanied. If he must have an escort, leave him alone – don't fuss! One has often noticed, by the way, that candidates who have to suffer the fussing process are generally those whose work would not be more than second-rate anyway.

Some youngsters come into the examination room with a cheerful smile – indeed, the majority in the elementary grades do. But some come in as if they were facing a major operation. They look at the exam-iner as if he were some fearsome monster thirsting for their blood. In many cases, as already suggested, this is the fault of teacher or parents. 'The examiner will be cross.' What the examiner likes is to see a smile – he tries to produce one himself – and a ready response to anything he may do in the hope of putting the candidate at his ease. To his cheerful 'Good morning' the re-action may be a frightened, dumb stare, and if he says something like, 'Make sure you're quite comfortable before you start', the candidate may shy like a startled fawn. This kind of thing, though not, admittedly, common, nevertheless does occur and is both distressing and irritating – and quite unnecessary. The child who has been properly trained and prepared comes in with a smile, settles down with ease and, we hope, leaves the room with another smile when the examination is over. The examination is not a trial to either party.

What we may call natural nervousness as opposed to that induced by outside influences is a different matter. Some candidates, even some whose work is fundamentally good, do tend to get 'worked up' and consequently do not perform at their best. The only ultimate cure is will-power plus concentration. The teacher must build up the pupil's self-confidence and try to make him believe in himself. The pupil must try to lose himself in the music and to put out of his mind that somebody is listening to him. This, certainly, is a counsel of perfection, but there is no other way. Not everybody realises that many of the greatest public performers are pitiably nervous before they go on to the platform. My own teacher told me of seeing Paderewski walking up and down in the artists' room before a recital, tearing his hair and wringing his hands in sheer funk. Yet to see him walk on to the platform one might have thought that there was not a nerve in his body. It was simply will-power. Occasionally one does meet with the pupil whose nerves just cannot be brought under control. Such cases are really unexaminable and it is far better never to enter them. But they are rare.

One of my colleagues has a pet saying, 'We don't fail the candidates, they fail themselves.' Allowing for one little matter, this is perfectly true and may well be carefully pondered by the reader. The little matter to be allowed for is that failure or a poor result may be as much due to the teacher as to the candidate. It has to be realised that not only is the candidate being examined, but also *the teacher through the candidate*. Apart from the odd slip, or trouble due to nervousness, weaknesses in the examination room are generally due to weaknesses in the actual teaching. If the examiner has reason to remark on a bad hand position or any other basic fault it is obviously the teacher who is to blame; the candidate does what he has been taught to do. (Compare what was said on page 17.) In such cases the teacher must blame himself, not the candidate or the examiner.

Another irritating remark which may arise from some comment made by the examiner is, 'Oh, don't you like it that way?' The candidate indulges in, say, a 'flapping' *staccato* action or something else which to the examiner is a basic fault. It is not a question of whether or not the examiner 'likes it that way' but rather of whether it is intrinsically good or bad. The examiner is not merely expressing his personal opinion that 'flapping' *staccato* is bad; he is stating a fact which his own training and experience have taught him and which is accepted by all competent teachers.

This leads to yet further remarks on the attitude to examinations and the examiner. If the teacher enters pupils for examinations he is, in doing so, implying that he is willing to accept the examiner's judgement as reliable. If he will not do this, if he wants to dispute this judgement, then why use the examinations at all? Examination syllabuses generally include a note that there is no appeal from the examiner's decision on any grounds whatever. Entry for the examination implies acceptance of this condition. It also implies admission that the examiner knows his job, so that disputing a decision, or the validity of a comment, is inadmissible.

The frequency with which examinations should be taken and the length of time to be spent in preparation must depend on the individual pupil. There is no harm in a yearly examination; indeed, the various grade syllabuses are based on this. The more gifted pupils are sometimes pushed into taking two grades in one year, which may or may not be a good thing.

It is in the time spent in preparation for any given examination that one finds so much bad method. During a three-year examination tour of India, for example, I very soon realised that if I examined and passed, say, five grade IV candidates on the 15th June, on the 16th they would be given two pieces and two studies for grade V, plus the additional scales and arpeggios, and would be kept at them and probably nothing else until I arrived on 15th June of the next year. This kind of thing is appalling, and it is not an exaggeration. Work for a future examination should not be confined to just two preselected pieces or studies. As much as possible of the material offered by the syllabus should be attempted, not necessarily up to concert pitch. The final selection should be made not more than three months before the examination and should take into account what seems to be best suited to the individual pupil. The early part of the year should be devoted to technical improvement, repertoire (not based solely on examination pieces), etc., with the intensive preparation beginning when the examination is actually coming into sight.

The general training must be such that an examination can be taken in the stride. One of the commonest weaknesses is to 'work up' to the required standard. This leaves no margin. Pupils should be brought well above the standard so that, for example, a pupil taking grade V should be capable of making a reasonable attempt at grade VI. This, obviously, can never be achieved working on the 'two studies, two pieces' principle mentioned above. Another obvious point none too often realised, is that if the pupil knows he is up to the standard of grade VI, grade V is not likely to worry him; he will know that he can take it in his stride and so will gain increased self-confidence.

On the matter of standard it must be pointed out that as we move up from grade to grade not only does the technical difficulty increase but also the requirements on the purely musical side. Musical development must run parallel to technical. That this is taken for granted by examining bodies is obvious enough from a glance through any syllabus, but it does need to be mentioned here. One finds a candidate taking, say, grade VI when technique is adequate enough but the musicianship is only about the level of grade II or III.

Careful selection of studies and pieces for the individual is, again, of the utmost importance, but is often not given enough attention. A pupil who can barely stretch an octave may present a piece with numerous full chords or 9th stretches; one whose finger-work is not well developed may present something consisting almost entirely of high-speed runs and so on. It is difficult to see why teachers do this sort of thing, but they do. Note, too, the matter of speed. If a finger study is marked, say, *allegro*, ♩ = 120. the examiner cannot give much credit if it is played *andante*, ♩ = 80 or less. The teacher may retort that it is better to achieve accuracy and fluency at the slower speed than to risk disaster at the higher. Quite. But why choose something which the pupil cannot manage up to speed? Syllabuses offer ample variety and it is never impossible to make a really appropriate choice for any given candidate.

Pupils must be made to understand clearly how the examination will be conducted – what they have to do and when to do it. Syllabuses state, 'The examination will be conducted in the order given in the syllabus', but some teachers never seem to read this sentence, or if they do, they never instruct their pupils accordingly. In the Trinity College grade II for example, the first things on the programme are the exercises. It is not unknown for the examiner to say, 'Comfortable? Right. Start from the beginning with the exercises' – and find himself presented with the scale of C major. This is not the fault of the candidate. He should be told something like this: 'Go up to the examiner and SMILE. Say good morning and hand him your card. Then get settled at the piano and when he tells you, begin the exercises. Scales come next and he'll tell you which ones he wants you to play. Then the studies and the pieces, and then he'll give you the sight reading and finally the aural tests. Say good-bye politely and come away'. Practise this order of procedure at lessons just before the examination so that the pupil becomes habituated to it.

Even diploma candidates are not guiltless in this matter. In the Trinity College associate and licentiate examinations the first item is the first piece. But one has told a candidate to start this piece and he has turned round and said, 'Which scale did you say?'

Two other small points. Occasionally a candidate may say, 'May I do the scales before the pieces?' or make some similar request. The examiner may choose to exercise his discretion but he is quite justified in insisting on adherence to the order given in the syllabus. Candidates occasionally play the second study or piece before the first for no reason except that they have apparently never been told that the first must come first. This is a mild irritation to the examiner.

It is accepted that the examiner may stop a performance as soon as he has heard enough to make his decision. Pupils should be made to understand that being stopped before the end does not necessarily mean that the performance is so bad that the examiner cannot bear to hear any more. It means simply that he has heard all he needs to.

Teachers and candidates must realise that the examiner has to work to a time-table. Some appear to think that he has unlimited time at his disposal for any

individual. He has not. Anything, therefore, that
wastes time is to be deprecated. It is not a matter of
wanting to rush the examination, but rather to keep
things moving steadily and easily. Some candidates
take an unconscionable time to get settled at the piano.
If their studies or pieces are in a volume, they never
mark the pages or remember their numbers, but spend
valuable time riffling them back and forth until the
right page is more or less accidentally found. There is
also the not uncommon candidate whose music is so
crumpled that it will not stand up. Alternatively it
may have been so bound up with sticky tape that it will
not stay open. With the exercise of a little common
sense, time-wasting things like these should never
occur, but they do.

One has suffered, too, from the violin or 'cello
candidate who brings his own collapsible music stand
but does not seem to know how to set it up; and the
teacher who needs anything up to ten minutes to tune
the instrument for a youngster. (This shows sheer
incompetence.) And the singing teacher preparing to
accompany her pupil, who has first to rummage through
an over-packed handbag to find her glasses, puts them
on, takes them off, wipes them, puts them on again,
holds a brief conversation with the pupil and when at
last she gets started either plays so heavily that the
voice is swamped, or plays so inaccurately that the
examiner's nerves are on edge – or both. All this, by
the way, is not apocryphal; it is taken from actual
experience, though admittedly it is not, luckily, too
common.

Another small point, but one which can be a
nuisance, is lack of clarity in speech, especially with
some youngsters. For example, in an aural test the
examiner plays a major chord, C, E, G, C, and then

replays one of the four notes, the candidate having to name it either by letter-name, number (1, 3, 5, 8) or Tonic solfa.   If the examiner plays G, the response may be something that sounds vaguely like 'Ee', so that he cannot know whether the candidate means G, or E, or Three, or Me.   I remember examining years ago in a town in Norfolk where dialect is apt at times to be pretty marked.   The test was, 'I'm going to play two notes and I want you to tell me whether the *second* note is higher or lower than the first.'   The reply from a small girl appeared to be 'Bomwom'.   It took several repetitions and much patience for me to realise that what she meant was 'bottom one', which presumably meant that the second note was the lower.   But why had she not been taught to say either 'higher' or 'lower'?

We now come to diploma examinations.   The first thing to realise is that a diploma is not just a matter of 'getting my letters' (a phrase which I admit annoys me intensely).   A diploma is a professional qualification and the examiner regards it as such, even if teachers and candidates do not.   If a student wants to achieve a teacher's diploma he must be able to satisfy the examiner not only that he can perform adequately, though not necessarily brilliantly, but that he is at least potentially a competent teacher.   Examining bodies cannot countenance the granting of teaching diplomas to people who obviously know nothing about teaching, in either its practical or theoretical aspects.   A performer's diploma does not necessarily demand that the candidate shall be a virtuoso, but he must be able to exhibit adequate technique and musicianship in his programme.

Too often the gap between the highest grade examination and the lowest diploma is not appreciated.   The difference between the standard required for a pass in grade VIII and that for a diploma is far greater than that between grades VII and VIII. The grade examination is purely for the student; the diploma is for the would-be professional. And even if a diploma is taken just for the experience, without any thought of professional teaching or of public performance, the same thing applies. The examiner cannot modify his standard according to individual circumstances.

If a pupil has worked through the grades at yearly intervals, he should allow, unless he is specially gifted, at least two years before attempting a diploma. He must allow, too, for the necessity of rest periods in the study of big works (see page 69). As with grade examinations, one finds too much 'working up' to what is considered to be a suitable standard with little or nothing in hand, and too much long-continued slogging away at selected pieces without a break. Study, put aside, study, put aside again and so on. Look well ahead.

A special word is needed regarding teacher's diploma examinations. As stated above, brilliant performance is not demanded (though there is no objection to it). But accuracy, well-founded and adequate technique, good musicianship and clear grasp are. Every branch of the examination must be handled at least competently. The examiner is not impressed by the candidate who can perform his pieces well enough yet makes a hopeless muddle of scales and arpeggios. Most important is the *viva voce*, since it is only in this that an opinion can be formed on the candidate's potentiality as a teacher. The examiner is not likely to ask questions on the more recondite aspects of technique such as arm *vibrato*. What he wants to find out is whether the candidate's ideas on the basic principles of teaching his subject are sound, whether he has an idea of well-planned method, and whether he can 'put it across'. Also, whether he can demonstrate.

Some candidates seem to rely on practically memorising books on teaching. It is, perhaps, mildly gratifying to ask, 'How would you set about teaching such-and-such?' and to be answered with a literal quotation from a book one has written oneself, but this means nothing. In the majority of cases the candidate cannot put the matter into his own words, still less can he *show* what has to be done and how to do it. Yet because he has been able to quote accurately from a book, he may be quite annoyed that he has failed through a poor *viva*. Mere book knowledge is not enough; there must be understanding and an ability to show the practical application.

Further, explanations must be simple and easily intelligible. Most young teachers are concerned with elementary work with young pupils. To say, for example, that to obtain *cantabile* tone on the piano (why not, for the child, singing tone?) we must 'depress the key gradually', as I have had said to me by more than one candidate, will convey nothing to any elementary pupil and precious little to a more advanced one. *Cantabile* is basically obtained by a weight touch. The approach to this has already been considered.

The examiner does not expect things to be explained in the words he would use himself, nor does he demand that demonstration should be exactly what he himself would do. He does expect a logical and well-ordered use of method and that this method shall be capable of producing the desired results. And that it shall be easily understood by young pupils.

To sum up the whole matter of the examiner's attitude to diplomas we may say that while he does not demand brilliant performance (though something approaching it is needed for the highest performer's diplomas), nor wide experience in teaching, he does expect the work to be of such quality that the holder of the diploma will not bring discredit on the institution which confers it.

Some notes on paper work examinations are desirable. Firstly, pupils must be taught to use their intelligence, to apply what they have learnt from text-books to the answering of questions. This is obvious enough but anyone who has marked papers knows that intelligence is at times far to seek.

The matters covered by the 'Rudiments of Music' are all purely mechanical, so that accuracy in working Rudiments papers depends largely on sheer memory, the more so in the very early grades. But mechanical memory alone is not sufficient; there must be real understanding. As long as a question appears in the form the pupil is used to, he can answer it correctly enough. But a new form of an old question may put him out of his stride, quite needlessly. Say 'write the scale of D major in semibreves' and he will give a correct answer. But rephrase it as 'write in semibreves the major scale which has a key-signature of two sharps', or 'of which the given note is the mediant' and it is a safe bet that at least a proportion of candidates will get into a tangle. Yet there is no fundamental difference in the meaning of the various ways of phrasing the question. Or again, 'name these intervals', giving each interval in a separate bar, causes no trouble. But if the examiner writes a melody in a certain key and asks 'name the intervals marked by brackets', a fair number of candidates will completely overlook the key-signature.

Part of the trouble in such cases as the above is due to over-insistence on mere rote-learning, essential though

it is, and lack of *intelligent* application.   Part is due to
working past papers (an excellent idea, of course) and
expecting the question on any given matter always to
appear in exactly the same form.   Whenever a new
form of an old question appears, still within the limits of
the syllabus, of course, the examining body will receive
a number of letters from indignant teachers complaining
that 'this has never been set before'.   Such complaints
are unjustifiable.   If the teaching were properly
comprehensive and intelligent, they would never
arise.

A frequent cause of needless worry is the omnibus
question, which deals with several different matters at
one time.   All that is needed is clear thinking and a
dissection of question into its component parts.   For
example: 'Write, in the tenor clef, in properly grouped
semiquavers in 6/8 time, one octave ascending and
descending of the melodic minor scale of G sharp,
without key-signature.   Complete the final bar with
rests in proper order.'
Dissection:
1. Tenor clef, not alto, soprano, etc.
2. Semiquavers in 6/8 time, which means two groups
   of six semiquavers in the bar.
3. One octave only.
4. Both ascending and descending, not ascending
   only.
5. Melodic minor, not harmonic, involving the
   sharpening of 6th and 7th degrees upwards and
   lowering them again downwards.
6. G *sharp* minor, five sharps, not G natural minor
   with two flats.   (This would be a certain mistake
   from a number of candidates.)
7. *Without* key-signature – but the signature must be
   known.

8. Complete the final bar in accordance with principles of grouping which should have been mastered long since, *and not forgotten.*

In inserting the necessary accidentals, the key-signature gives F sharp, but F being the seventh note of the scale it has to be sharpened ascending, F double-sharp (*not G natural!*).   In 6/8 semiquavers, the first few notes of the descending scale will come in the same bar as the ascending one, so care must be taken over the accidentals for the lowered 7th and 6th degrees.   The only other matter is direction of stems, again according to rules which should have been learnt long before.

All the above may seem very obvious, but pupils need to be trained to work step by step on the right lines.

One could list literally scores of silly little mistakes which teachers themselves appear to condone or overlook.   The two dots of the bass clef, one on each side of the fourth line of the stave (not the third, or no dots at all), * accidentals not on the same line or space as the notes to which they are supposed to refer, the use of ## for double-sharp, and so on.   Attention to every detail is essential.

The study of harmony, counterpoint, etc., postulates the ability to hear mentally (see Chapter VII) and without this ability no great progress can be made, nor any great success expected in written examinations, however much use may be made of 'stock phrases' and however much care may be exercised in the avoidance of grammatical errors such as consecutives.   Apart from this, there is nothing much to say except to give a warning to read the question properly.   So often in the higher grade papers one finds a three-part question worked in four parts – careless reading.   The same

* Does the teacher know the origin of the dots? And if so, does he pass this knowledge on to his pupils?

applies in papers on teaching, form and history. The question must be read through more than once to decide exactly what is required. For example, a question on the sonata (as a whole) may be answered incompletely in terms of sonata (first movement) form; one on sonata form in terms of the sonata as a whole. This particular form of foolishness, by the way, is not unknown in degree examinations.

Further, especially in teaching papers, it is desirable to argue from the general to the particular, unless the question clearly demands particularisation. A question on the teaching of time may be answered solely in terms of 2/4, whereas the main body of the answer should cover the matter in general terms, using 2/4, or some other time-signature, as a specific example to show the application of the general principles. Knowledge of the syllabus is also needed. For example, the syllabus for the Trinity College associate 'Principles of Teaching' paper, and reference to past papers, make it quite clear that question 2 always deals with aural training in some form or other. Yet if the question asks, 'How would you teach the recognition of the major and the minor 3rd?' without actually using the word 'aurally', some candidates are certain to deal with the matter from the 'rudiments' angle, completely disregarding the aural.

All the above should be perfectly obvious, but experience shows that to many people it is far from being so. Yet it is all just plain common sense.

X

Musical Appreciation

THE average teacher, who probably deals entirely with individual pupils, may perhaps consider this chapter redundant since Appreciation is one of the few branches of music study which can be and generally is dealt with in class fashion. He may also ask how he can be expected to add Appreciation to the already crowded lesson. True enough. But every teacher should be an 'Appreciationist' in that he should try to inculcate in his pupils a love for and understanding of good music. His aim must be that whatever the circumstances and however limited the available time, they must enjoy their music.

Appreciation cannot be 'taught' any more than Composition; it must be cultivated and fostered. But unless we narrow down the meaning of the term to a mere dissection and analysis of compositions, teaching in the accepted sense of the word is impossible.

It is first necessary to decide on what we mean by Appreciation and on what should be its object. Despite the requirements of some examination syllabuses, it does not, as suggested above, mean only dissection and structural analysis, however desirable these may be for the more advanced student. Appreciation, which should be cultivated through the ear rather than through the eye, should, again as suggested above, aim at love, enjoyment (in the widest sense of the word) and understanding of music. There is no harm at all in the pupil knowing how phrases are built up into sentences and sentences into paragraphs, or the outlines of the various musical forms. But far more important is that he should be sufficiently appreciative to sit back and say, 'That's a jolly fine tune.' Dissection and analysis may be to the taste of one who is born with the mind and outlook of the embryo musicologist, but they are apt to be toil and tribulation to the average youngster. The pupil who can, to put it colloquially, get a kick out of his music is much farther along the road to musical salvation than he who can only analyse more or less mathematically the structure of a movement in sonata form but on whom the music makes no sensuous or emotional impression. (One has known not a few learned doctors of music of this latter type. To them such a work as the Fifth Symphony of Beethoven is little more than a masterpiece of musical design; they can expatiate at length on its use of germinal themes, on the innovations it contains, on everything, in fact, except the beauty and meaning of the music itself.)

In the essay 'Music and Musical Criticism' in his *Studies in Modern Music*,* Sir Henry Hadow distinguishes three ways in which 'we are ordinarily influenced by music', in other words, three aspects of its appreciation, *viz.* the sensuous, the emotional and the intellectual.

The first he defines as 'the purely physical, the effect of bodily pleasure or pain, which is produced on the nervous system by a concurrence or succession of air vibrations . . . analogous to those impressions of the palate which are translated into taste, or to those movements of the optic nerve which are translated into colour'. This is usually regarded as the least developed

---

* Seeley, Service & Co. Ltd. Published as far back as 1893 so that to the author, 'modern music' included such composers as Berlioz and Schumann. Nevertheless, the book is well worth the attention of any present-day musician.

kind of appreciation, to be interpreted as the pleasure (or lack of it) that we experience from the mere sound of a thing.

The second Hadow defines as 'the semi-physical in which, for the mere corporeal excitation of the senses, we have that subtler and more sublimated form of influence which it is usual to comprise under the name of emotion'. This comes into play when we find that a melody 'moves us' in some way or other, or when we find ourselves stirred or uplifted by some magnificent passage.

With regard to the intellectual aspect he says: 'Third, and most vital of the three, is the rational or logical side, through which we appraise an artistic work, not by any test of sensuous pleasure or emotional stimulus, but by some definite and intelligible scheme of aesthetic laws. To this belongs our appreciation of style, our appreciation of structure, all that we really imply in the word "criticism".'

It must be understood that Hadow was writing for the educated musician, not for the beginner; nevertheless, all that he says has relevance to our present purpose.

The child's appreciation of music (unless he happens to be a second Mozart) is purely sensuous. He 'likes the sound' of a thing – or he does not. (Some grown-ups progress little if anything beyond this point.) It is, therefore, the teacher's job to lead him onwards to the second stage. Obviously the music used, whether for performance study or simply for listening, must have sensuous appeal; its idiom must be one with which the child will feel at home, as must also its sound as such, and the utmost care must be exercised over its choice. It is here that some teachers adopt a wrong approach, an approach sometimes conditioned far too much by their own tastes, taking insufficient account of the tastes and mentality of the pupils or of their lack of musical background and development.

I recall a young man who was awaiting appointment as a music master at a big public school, whom I was questioning in a degree *viva voce*. I asked him what kind of material he would use in Appreciation classes for, say, eleven-year-olds and all he would propose were 'the Purcell Suite dances' (which he would probably have insisted should be played on a harpsichord!). A suggestion that these might not be the most easily approachable and assimilable things in the circumstances was rejected almost with scorn; neither my two colleagues nor I could get him away from his 'Purcell Suite dances'. Yet what interest the average boy of eleven (and it is the average, not the exceptional, that has to be considered) would find in them is difficult to discover – with all due respect to Purcell. If we want to introduce youngsters to keyboard music, pieces like the 'Military' Polonaise of Chopin (despite its noisiness and tendency to vulgarity), or Schumann's 'Träumerei', or Weber's 'Moto Perpetuo' (which appeals through its high-speed brilliance) are far more to the point.

In choosing music for Appreciation, it is necessary to take into account that most if not all children perforce hear a great deal of what cannot by any stretch of imagination be called 'good' music. There is a continual barrage of 'pop stuff' from radio, television, in restaurants, etc., and the harmful influence of this has to be counteracted as much as possible. 'Good', however, does not necessarily mean 'highbrow' but rather 'good of its kind'. For which reason, light music should not be despised. A good waltz is worth half a dozen bad symphonies and even if the young listener never gets beyond the stage of appreciating a waltz by Johann Strauss or a march by Elgar or Eric Coates, he will at least have made contact with something really worth while.

Some teachers, especially the younger ones who have not long completed their studentship at a college of music, tend to look down on anything which is not highbrow and to deprecate the use of light music as a means of introducing children to something better than 'pop'. They may well be reminded of what happened when Johann Strauss asked Brahms for his autograph. Brahms, with the reputation of a rather crusty old bachelor, moving in the elevated atmosphere of his magnificent symphonies and chamber music, wrote the opening bars of the 'Blue Danube' waltz and added below, 'Not, unfortunately, by Johannes Brahms.' Note the 'unfortunately'. Brahms himself produced his sets of Hungarian dances which are far from highbrow, not to mention his 'Liebeslieder' waltzes. Schubert, the composer of such tremendous (not to say terrifying) songs as 'Erlkönig' and 'Der Doppelgänger', wrote a number of delightful *Ländler* which are, quite simply, light music (and which, in the hands of a really fine artist, are a wonderful experience).

In the essay mentioned above, Hadow says 'there are thousands of people who "hate classical music". If by "classical music" is meant the work of all the greatest composers indiscriminately, then there is only one reason why people should hate it, namely that they have not heard it properly'. The writer might equally well have said that they have probably hardly heard it at all – they have never given it a chance. The same applies at times in the case of non-'classical' music; the serious student (and how serious the professional student can be!) decides that it is beneath his notice.

Some years ago I made some casual remark to a very earnest young degree student about Elgar's 'Pomp and Circumstance' marches and was rewarded with a sniff and a comment which savoured of 'Pooh – that rubbish'. So I arranged to give an illustrated talk to the college students on light music in general, and on musical snobbery. The programme included various dances by Strauss and similar composers. After it was over, students came to me and said, 'That was marvellous – we'd no idea. If only we could have cleared the chairs away and danced.' Even my serious-minded young man had to admit that he was converted.

If the student has reached the stage when he can really appreciate good light music, he can then be led further by way of what are generally called 'light classics'. Here again the emphasis must at first be on the 'light'. It is no use going straight from Strauss or Lehar or Eric Coates to the G minor Symphony of Mozart – and I have even had a young teacher tell me that he would use this last work as a *beginning* for Appreciation. The music must be tuneful and have obvious appeal, both sensuous and emotional; it must be essentially 'simple' in its meaning. Mozart, of course, need not be neglected, but it must rather be the Mozart of 'Eine Kleine Nachtmusik' or the Haffner Serenade, both of which the composer would have considered 'light'.

Not long before writing this book I attended a youth orchestral concert the programme of which included, among one or two other none-too-simple works, the Sixth Symphony of Sibelius – a work which the experienced musician needs to study deeply before he can begin to appreciate its meaning and message. The audience consisted largely of teenage school-children, all keen enough and many of them well primed in advance by their teachers. Reception was cool and a local critic complained bitterly of this, demanding, 'What do these young people want?' What they wanted and what they needed at their stage of musical development was very evident at a later concert in the same series, at which the programme consisted of a Rossini overture, the Tchaikovsky Violin Concerto, Mendelssohn's 'Italian' Symphony and Berlioz's Hungarian March. Not, perhaps, a programme for the dedicated highbrow, but its reception showed that the music had hit home – it was enjoyed and appreciated.

In the end it all boils down to the simple fact that the young listener has to learn to walk before he can run. The teacher (or the concert promoter) must as it were dangle the carrot in front of the donkey's nose – not that this is intended to suggest that the listener is necessarily asinine!

Equal care is needed in dealing with the really young, whether in connection with Appreciation or the songs they may sing in class. Appreciation enters, obviously if indirectly, into the latter. The child's early contacts with music must be such that he will sing or otherwise experience music which, however elementary, is good of its kind and which is attractive at his current stage of development. Insistence on a lot of folk-songs is not always wise; it depends on the songs themselves. There is a type of mind which will accept any folk-song as good simply because it is a folk-song, but this attitude is misguided. Some such songs are not particularly good music and some, except to the dedicated 'folkists', are frankly dull. Musically speaking, dullness is an unforgivable crime.

It may be well, too, to mention that not every work by a 'great' composer is good just because it happens to have been written by him. Every great composer has written a proportion of music which is not worth bothering about, but there are those who are far from willing to admit this. Beethoven, or Mozart, or Wagner wrote it, therefore it must be good. But Beethoven was not always writing up to the standard of the Fifth Symphony or the 'Appassionata' Sonata (he wrote, among other things, that dreadful 'Battle' Symphony); Mozart at times fell far below the incredible perfection of the G minor Quintet or the 'Jupiter' Symphony; Wagner was capable of scraping the bottom of the barrel of sheer vulgarity. And the same applies to other composers. Admitted that some works are unduly neglected and when taken off the shelf by some enlightened conductor or performer prove to contain unexpected delights. There are, for example, early symphonies by Mozart and Schubert which are hardly known, yet are full of beauty. But generally speaking the concert repertoire, from which the teacher will naturally draw his appreciation repertoire, contains most of the works which are really worth performing. (A recent hearing of Tchaikovsky's first three symphonies made it very clear why only the fourth, fifth and sixth are normally played.)

Reference may also be made to hackneyed works. Why does a work become hackneyed – hackneyed, that is, to the superior person who thinks he knows it too well? Generally it is because it is so good that people want to hear it again and again; it has permanent appeal. Beethoven's Fifth Symphony, Schubert's 'Unfinished', Bach's 'Jesu, Joy of man's desiring' are all hackneyed from one point of view, but are they any the worse music for that? However well we may know them we can always afford to know them better, and each hearing deepens our understanding and insight.

This leads to a comment on the importance of repeated hearings, though obviously repetitions must not be too frequent. No great work can be properly appreciated at a single hearing, however immediate its appeal. However well we may think we know a work, there is always something to learn about it. Quoting once again from my own experience, I once made an orchestral arrangement of Bach's great organ Prelude and Fugue in B minor, a work I had known and played for forty years and of which I could have written out the organ score from memory. As I worked on the orchestral score I found myself almost humiliated as I realised how much of its inner detail and texture I had not properly appreciated before.

The really great works will always thrill, even though one knows all the time what is coming. Think, for example, of the passage which joins the third and fourth movements of Beethoven's Fifth Symphony. We may know well enough that the mysterious creeping about over the long pedal will lead to a sudden *crescendo* into the finale, but if we have any musical sensibility at all, how can we avoid a mental shout of triumph when this *crescendo* achieves its climax on the chord of C major? Or, at the other end of the scale, how can we not find ourselves uplifted to the highest degree at 'Truly this was the Son of God' in the *St. Matthew Passion*, even at the twentieth – or hundredth – hearing?

Turning now to Hadow's third aspect of appreciation, the intellectual, it may be frankly admitted that not many, apart from highly trained professionals, can achieve it to any great extent. It demands long and intensive study of many branches of music – harmony, form, the orchestra, musical history, aesthetics and so on. Nevertheless, even a modest amount of such knowledge will help towards a keener and deeper appreciation of music, always provided that there is already developed appreciation at the two lower levels and that the dissection-analysis aspect is not considered the only one that really matters. Even a fairly elementary understanding of the principles of musical design will lead to a clearer grasp of the composer's aims, as will also an outline knowledge of the history of music. How many teachers ever bother to explain to their pupils *why* Bach and his contemporaries wrote so many fugues, whereas Haydn, Mozart, Beethoven and their fellows wrote such a preponderance of works of the sonata type? Still more to the point, how many teachers explain that to Bach a fugue was not just an exercise in advanced contrapuntal writing (in which generations of examination candidates struggle more or less unsuccessfully with the problems of part-playing!) but a means of personal expression? (And it is worth mentioning that some of Bach's fugues which are the most complex contrapuntally are also those which are most intensely emotional. See, for example, the C sharp minor and E flat minor of book 1 of the 'Forty-eight'.)

What the teacher must do, therefore, is to build up in his pupils, whether in appreciation classes or otherwise, a liking for good music of all kinds, to foster their ability to enjoy and understand it. As they progress he may introduce the more intellectual approach, as far as their musical and general mental development will permit. But he must never lose sight of the fact that the pupil should learn to look upon music not simply as a matter of study, but as a vital factor in his life – and that good music is good fun.

XI

Conclusion

THE underlying themes of this book, as will be realised by those who read it intelligently, are three — work hard, use your brains, and aim always for the highest. Sincere and honest teaching is an exhausting business; the teacher is 'giving out' all the time. But he must never relax, never 'let up'. And incidentally, he should never natter at his pupils. Censure may at times be necessary, but it should not savour of nagging.

A good teacher can exercise a big influence on the character of his pupils, not merely in connection with music. The pupil who is trained always to aim at the highest in his music study, to strive always for perfection, is likely to adopt the same attitude to other work. Slackness in the teacher inevitably results in slackness in the pupil. Music study properly pursued is a means of mental development.

The importance of breadth in the training cannot be over-emphasised. Whatever may be the attitude of the parents, or of the pupils themselves, we must never be content merely to teach on the 'two studies, two pieces' principle (if it can be called a principle). We must do all we can to open the minds of our pupils to music in the wider sense, to give them, as far as their own mentality will permit, some feeling for and understanding of its beauty. And we must aim to inculcate the feeling that the study of music can be and should be good fun.

124